"In *The Chinese Way*, Betty Liu showcases a familiar mode of cooking in our family—applying Chinese techniques and a search for vibrantly varied textures and flavors to both traditional and non-traditional ingredients. Her inventive recipes show us that 'cooking Chinese' is an ethos that any home cook can learn. This book is a joy to read and cook from!"
—Kaitlin, Sarah, Bill, and Judy Leung,
*New York Times* bestselling authors of *The Woks of Life*

"Betty Liu's clever new cookbook is Chinese cooking gone wild! She first teaches the traditional recipes and then shows the fun and delicious variations you can create when you understand the basics. Once you cook recipes like Sriracha Shrimp Toast, Sesame Cumin Fried Chicken, or Garlicky Radicchio and Pork Stir-Fry, this way of thinking about Chinese culinary techniques will inspire your own creativity!"
—Grace Young,
author of *Stir-Frying to the Sky's Edge*

"*The Chinese Way* is destined to be one of my most used cookbooks—I cannot stop cooking from it! Betty takes Chinese cooking fundamentals and effortlessly applies them into everyday dishes that are approachable, familiar, and inspired. Stunning photography and whimsically informative illustrations make every page of this book worthy of exploration. It's a joyful homage to everyday Chinese cooking."
—Alana Kysar,
author of the bestselling cookbook *Aloha Kitchen*

# THE CHINESE WAY

BETTY LIU

# THE CHINESE WAY

## CLASSIC TECHNIQUES, FRESH FLAVORS

Photographs by Betty Liu | Illustrations by Justine Wong

VORACIOUS

Little, Brown and Company
New York | Boston | London

To Alex and Emmett,
my true loves, and to
my mom and dad, who are
endlessly inspirational

# INTRODUCTION
## BREAK DOWN THE BARRIERS

When I first moved away from home and craved the Chinese food I grew up with, I called my mom to ask how to make tomato and egg, the quintessential home-style Chinese dish. She launched into a monologue, which wasn't quite a recipe, but did convey the steps and concepts of how to make the dish. Eventually I figured out enough to cobble together something that, while edible, wasn't quite the same. The next time I visited home and watched her cook, I took a video, so I could transcribe the recipe for myself later. I still call her to ask how she makes certain dishes—most recently, the pork and onion baos she and my dad concocted while she was here during my postpartum recovery—and though she hasn't changed the way she describes the cooking process, I find that I'm able to decipher her instructions. The difference is, I think, that my own cooking skills and intuition have evolved. I now speak her cooking language.

It's a common trope that generational cooking passes down without a written recipe. In my experience, this is true. My mom never works from a recipe. She draws on her own experiences cooking with her Shanghainese family and re-creates dishes from her taste memories. As with any prolonged game of Telephone, the message inevitably changes and transforms.

These differences between the original recipe and its subsequent iterations are not about inaccuracy. They reveal the fluidity of food.

Like my mom, I cook Chinese all the time, but that doesn't mean we make the same food my great-grandparents did. Of course we love the traditional dishes, especially for special occasions. My mom's 红烧肉 hóng shāo ròu, red-braised pork belly, is the best, as are her shāo mài, chive cakes, and stir-fried crab. These dishes hold a special place in my heart, evoking not only the memory that is shaped by my palate, but also the remembrance of the warmth of my mom's kitchen, that specific feeling of arriving home.

Yet the hóng shāo ròu I make in my Boston kitchen isn't exactly the same as the one my mom makes in her California kitchen, which isn't exactly the same as her parents made in Shanghai. Dishes evolve.

This book is about the way I cook Chinese food every day. It's not traditional, but it is Chinese.

When I write about Chinese food, I try to avoid using the word "authentic," because it is impossible to apply broadly. If you poll various Chinese individuals who grew up in the same region about a certain dish, I guarantee you each will have their own personal taste memory of that dish—what is authentic to them. My way isn't—and shouldn't be—your way. When my mom throws together a stir-fry with the Western ingredients chard and fennel, is this not Chinese cooking? You can cook Chinese without being Chinese. You can cook Chinese without a Chinese kitchen. You can cook Chinese without using specific brands of soy sauce.

As a second-generation Chinese American living on the East Coast, I don't cook strictly traditional recipes every day at home. Most Chinese Americans don't. Instead, I use a mishmash of traditional and modern tools and ingredients. I have access to a Chinese grocery store, and I also shop at H Mart (the Korean grocery chain), Trader Joe's, and Whole Foods. I order foods from all over the world from online marketplaces. I have bottles of Kimlan soy sauce sitting next to a well-used box of English Maldon flaky sea salt. I have preserved lemons in a jar. Sambal oelek, with its green lid, is in my fridge. So is concentrated tomato paste in a tube, along with kimchi, two types of miso, Parmigiano-Reggiano cheese, and a jar of giardiniera (Italian pickled mixed vegetables) made by my friend's family in Chicago. I cherish my Fly By Jing Zhong Sauce, which sits next to my homemade **Fried Shallot Chile Crisp (page 207).**

My carbon-steel wok, which I lugged all the way from Shanghai, sits comfortably over the range next to my Dutch oven, my beloved cast-iron pans, and my nonstick skillet. I use a cleaver, cooking chopsticks, and a wok frequently. I roast food in my oven, and a Chinese bamboo steamer sits on my stovetop. I drink coffee in the morning and jasmine green tea in the afternoon. I'm influenced by culinary greats from Yotam Ottolenghi to Samin Nosrat, and Hetty McKinnon to Joshua McFadden.

What ties all these influences together and makes the food that I cook "Chinese" is technique. Whether I'm stir-frying cauliflower or adding preserved lemon to broccoli for some extra zing, I am drawing from a foundation of Chinese cooking that has been passed down for generations. This approach showcases modern cooking, but it's still quintessentially Chinese. In fact, incorporating local produce and flavors while using traditional techniques is the essence of Chinese regional cooking.

In writing this book, I wanted to break down the mental barriers to cooking Chinese. There is no one way to make each dish. If an ingredient is too hard to source, then omit it. Chinese cooking is not a set of rules with strict, by-the-book recipes. Instead, it's forgiving, flexible, and entirely applicable to your pantry, because the Chinese way of cooking is really about adaptability.

The flavors in this book are still largely Asian, though not always traditional. They are an amalgam of my personal experiences in the kitchen: my childhood in a Chinese immigrant household in the Bay Area in a largely Asian community, my college years in St. Louis, my travels, and my adult years undergoing medical training in Boston.

## SEE ONE, DO ONE, TEACH ONE

The first kitchen skill I learned was how to pare an apple. When I showed interest in wanting to help in the kitchen, my dad grabbed an apple and guided me through peeling the skin. My goal quickly became trying to pare an apple in one swoop, ending up with an unbroken, long, swirling peel. This taught me a few things: how to hold a paring knife, to be cognizant of the sharp blade, to get a kinesthetic sense of where my thumb was in relation to the blade, and to feel the nuances in the blade pressure for different varieties of apples. From this one exercise, I started to learn how to prepare food.

In my surgical training, there is a teaching mantra: *see one, do one, teach one.* As a trainee, you observe a procedure. You perform one. Then, you lead another junior trainee through that same procedure. In reality, of course, it takes more than just one observation and one procedure to acquire the skills necessary to teach the

procedure, but with each level, you gain a different perspective and skill set that will ultimately lead to mastery.

And thus, the structure of this book took shape.

It is divided into the eight fundamental Chinese cooking techniques: steam, fry, boil, braise, sauce, infuse, pickle, and wrap. Within each technique, there may be subcategories. Within Fry, for

example, there are stir-fry and deep-fry, just as Boil includes other water-based techniques like simmer. The first four chapters—Steam, Fry, Boil, and Braise—are about cooking with different forms of heat. (These techniques, of course, often overlap in a single recipe.) The next four chapters—Sauce, Infuse, Pickle, and Wrap— are about putting food combinations together.

I encourage you to see the instructions in the recipes as a starting point, a launch pad for your cooking adventures. In making the recipes, you are adding to your fund of knowledge; your instinct is developed by doing. It's similar to the way a dish is passed down by word of mouth rather than by a written recipe. After you've cooked your way through this book, you'll feel more comfortable throwing together a fast stir-fry, whipping out your steamer, or sizzling aromatics for a topping using what you have in your pantry or fridge. With an understanding of core Chinese home-cooking techniques, you'll set yourself up for success to make good food the Chinese way.

## ABOUT THE RECIPES

I tend to use weights when I cook because they're more accurate than measuring by volume, though I recognize that volume is more common. For major ingredients in larger quantities, I've included both measures. For doughs, where precision really matters, I recommend measuring by weight.

My serving sizes are simply a guide. That's because the Chinese way to eat is usually family style. There are no individual portions served—the dishes are placed in the middle of the table and shared among a few people. Then, too, appetites vary greatly. For example, I can eat eight wontons in one serving, but my husband, Alex, can easily down twenty. So one dish may not by itself serve four comfortably, but is meant to be eaten alongside other dishes for four.

I love substitutions and encourage you to explore them. When you substitute, pay attention to your ingredient and adjust the recipe accordingly. For example, if you use maple syrup instead of granulated sugar, you'll need to keep in mind that maple syrup has an intrinsic flavor, and as a liquid, will add volume.

One core technique at a time, you'll learn about the underlying principles. I start with a few traditional recipes to highlight how a particular method has been used. In the remainder of the chapter, nontraditional recipes demonstrate how the technique can be used in different ways, without the at-times-intimidating confines of tradition.

# THE MODERN CHINESE PANTRY

The first time I tried to stock a pantry, I was in college, living in a dorm. This meant my ingredients were limited to a box I could lug from my room to the communal kitchen and back. I remember calling my mom and keeping her on the line as I perused the tiny Chinese grocery store in St. Louis, asking her where I should start. I grabbed soy sauce, black vinegar, Shaoxing wine, sugar, and some dried wheat noodles. That was it. Salt and black pepper were available in the communal kitchen (sometimes still in their little paper packets).

Over time, things have changed—not just for me, but for my mother as well. When she came to Boston from California to cook for me after I had my baby, she used my light and dark soy sauces (which she had counseled me to buy years ago), but when it came time to restock, chose the Japanese soy sauce that she now uses for everything. Cooking methods, taste preferences, and therefore the contents of the pantry change.

Over anything else, make sure your ingredients are high quality and therefore flavorful. The markets in China are extremely fresh, and farmers' markets open daily. In the Chinese farmer's almanac, there are twenty-four distinct seasons—a hint about how important seasonality is to agriculture there. Produce bought in the morning is used that night.

Know your preferences and those of the people you cook for. For this book, my **Mapo Tofu (page 134)** was tested by a few different people, and therefore made with various sets of chile peppers, red pepper flakes, and doubanjiang. The feedback I received ranged from "this is quite spicy compared to mapo tofu I've had before" to "this isn't spicy enough," even though each tester followed the same set of instructions.

Assess your spices. Favor quality over quantity. **See page 20** for how I manage my dry spices.

I've organized these ingredients, including staples and specialty ingredients, by broad flavor profiles, so that you can start to think about them not only in terms of what the ingredients are, but how they can balance a dish. Harder to describe, though equally important, is the texture of these ingredients—something crunchy but acidic will contribute something very different than something creamy and acidic.

# 咸 xián (salty)

## SOY SAUCES • SALTS • FISH SAUCE • CHEESE
## CURED MEATS • MISO • DOENJANG • OYSTER SAUCE • DASHI

There is a lot of overlap between salty and umami, so please take my categorizations with—pardon the pun—a grain of salt. When I started exploring Western cooking, one of the first lessons I heard was to season at every step. This felt very familiar to me, since the Chinese way of cooking involves seasoning throughout the cooking process. It doesn't mean seasoning at literally every step (for example, when frying garlic, ginger, and scallion, it's not necessary to add seasoning). Instead, remember that seasoning shouldn't happen all at once at the end. It should be a natural, instinctive, incorporated part of your process—inseparable from cooking. Think about whether seasoning is appropriate in prepping, saucing, cooking, and finishing (hint: the answer is usually yes).

**SOY SAUCE** (酱油 *jiàng yóu*) is my favorite salty ingredient for seasoning. Since it's a liquid, it incorporates easily, and it has more than just salty flavors, with depth and umami, due to its fermenting process.

• **Light soy sauce** (生抽 *shēng chōu*) will contribute umami saltiness to your cooking. Light soy sauce is more salty than dark soy sauce, and I use this regularly for seasoning. Kimlan and Pearl River Bridge are my go-to brands.

• **Dark soy sauce** (老抽 *lǎo chōu*) is slightly thicker and will contribute more deep brown color to your cooking, as well as provide some subtle molasses notes.

• **Tamari,** a byproduct of miso, is a type of Japanese soy sauce without the presence of wheat, which is used in the fermentation process for traditional soy sauce. It is dark and still fragrant, but a bit less salty. I tend to use tamari now because my son was diagnosed with a wheat allergy, and it has been extremely easy to adapt. Because it is slightly less salty, I add a splash more to my dishes, and as always, adjust by taste.

**SALT**

• **Kosher salt** is my go-to for seasoning. Taste your food throughout the cooking process and adjust to your preference. The recipes in this book were tested with Diamond Crystal kosher salt.

• **Flaky salt**, such as Maldon sea salt, is handy to have on hand for a final sprinkle (and crunch).

• **Fish sauce** is salty with a fishy umami flavor, in the best way possible. Just a splash can add a punch to your cooking.

**CHEESES** such as pecorino or Parmigiano-Reggiano add both creaminess and a savory flavor. I keep a block of Parmigiano-Reggiano to grate. Keep the rinds to infuse into soup, like **Hearty Bean-Broth Udon Noodle Soup, page 202.**

**CURED MEATS** like Spam, bacon, salt pork, pancetta, or prosciutto have concentrated salty and deep porky flavors due to their curing and aging process. Each has its own advantages and methods of cooking—for example, Spam is great seared with a splash of soy sauce to get a caramelized layer, whereas bacon contributes a generous rendering of fat.

**MISO** (fermented soybean paste) is a staple umami-rich seasoning in Japanese cooking. Keep an eye out for different varieties of miso, based on the grain used in the fermentation process—barley miso, for example, has a gorgeous nutty flavor that makes a great soup very quickly.

**DOENJANG** (Korean fermented soybean paste) has an earthy, savory flavor; you can use it like miso.

**OYSTER SAUCE** or **ABALONE SAUCE** are both salty, sweet, and umami, adding a bit of mild fishiness to a dish.

**DASHI** (or **HONDASHI**) is made from dried kombu and dried fish such as bonito flakes. Slightly ocean-y, savory, with a complex deliciousness that makes you want to smack your lips, a splash of this stock can add depth to your sauces, braises, or stir-fries. Use it in **Dashi-Steamed Mushrooms (page 48)** for a double umami dish. I've included instructions in the recipe for making a classic dashi, but you can also reconstitute dashi powder.

# 鲜 xiān
# (umami deliciousness)

## BLACK GARLIC • FURU • FERMENTED BLACK BEANS
## DOUBANJIANG • SHACHA SAUCE

In the Chinese dictionary, 鲜 *xiān* means fresh, but when it is used in the context of flavor, its meaning is more complex. I asked my dad to translate the word, and he said "deliciousness." Similarly, umami in Japanese stems from the Japanese words for delicious and taste. It describes a complex, savory deliciousness, like a perfectly seasoned pure broth—"好鲜! So delicious!" you exclaim.

**DRIED INGREDIENTS** not only last for a while in your pantry, but due to their dehydrated state, hold a wealth of concentrated flavor.
• **Dried mushrooms,** including shiitake mushrooms, have umami flavor that is deepened and concentrated in the dehydrated caps, and can be easily unlocked by pouring hot (not boiling) water over them. The water is thus infused with the mushroom flavor, earthy and savory, to be used as a stock in your cooking. Dried shiitakes are graded for quality. You want to keep an eye out for the ones called 花菇 *huā gū* (flower mushrooms), due to the floral pattern on the cap. Another great dried mushroom is the 木耳 *mù ěr* (wood ear): slippery, wavy, thin mushrooms that have a surprising crunch and are delicious in stir-fries. They come in compact dried form and expand quite a bit when rehydrated in hot water.
• **Dried shrimp** (虾米 *xiā mǐ*) are versatile little flavor bombs that can be sprinkled into soups, stir-fries, or braises. They are tiny—the size of corn kernels—and dehydrated, with a concentrated umami shrimpy flavor. Rehydrate by soaking in hot water or Shaoxing wine.

- **Dried scallops** (干贝 *gān bèi*) are prized for their savory, fishy flavor. A little goes a long way.
- **Dried fish** such as salted yellow croaker or Japanese bonito flakes can add a lot of umami.

**BLACK GARLIC** adds a funky, amplified garlic flavor—a delightful addition to your umami toolbox. See how it can power the flavor behind **Cod with Black Garlic Butter (page 60).**

**FURU** (豆腐乳 *dòu fǔ rǔ*) or fermented tofu comes in a spicy red or salty white brine. These little wobbly cubes are akin to blue cheese, with a funkiness that can be an acquired taste. A little can impart strong flavor—I love taking a little chunk of it with the tips of my chopsticks and eating it with something plain, like an unseasoned congee. Add it to your sauces and dressings and experience how this can add an extra layer of umami.

**FERMENTED BLACK BEANS** (豆豉 *dòu chǐ*) are shriveled, pitch-black soybeans that have been allowed to cure and ferment. They pack a funky punch. The unique salty, umami flavor is impossible to describe. It is worth getting some just to experience their fragrance and see how they can be transformed with heat in a dish.

**DOUBANJIANG** (豆瓣酱 *dòu bàn jiàng*) or fermented broad bean paste is fava beans fermented with chiles. It's from Sichuan and it has a strong, salty, spicy, funky flavor. It's the foundation of **Mapo Tofu (page 134).** For the best-quality doubanjiang, look for ones from Pixian, a city just outside Chengdu. Also pay attention to the color of the paste: a darker amber hue means a more aged paste and thus a more complex, deep flavor. A great aged doubanjiang is available via Fly By Jing.

**SHACHA SAUCE** (沙茶酱 *shā chá jiàng*) is a concoction of alliums, chiles, dried shrimp, and dried fish—a bunch of umami ingredients combined into a single condiment. My go-to dipping sauce for hot pot is a mix of fresh garlic, fresh scallions, and shacha sauce.

# 甜 tián (sweet)

**HONEY • DARK BROWN SUGAR • GRANULATED SUGAR MAPLE SYRUP • COARSE RAW SUGAR • ROCK SUGAR • HOISIN SAUCE CARAMELIZED ONIONS OR SHALLOTS • JAMS**

I am very Shanghainese in this way: I keep a little dish of sugar right next to my dish of kosher salt and my black pepper in a peppermill by the stove. Salt and pepper are hailed as a pair, but let me counter with this trio: salt, sugar, black pepper. Sugar is vital in cooking, as it will balance saltiness, spiciness, and acidity. There are so many sweeteners you can use. With each, consider what form (crystal, powder, liquid) it comes in, if it needs to be dissolved, and its intrinsic flavor profile.

**HONEY** works great in sauces since it's already in liquid form. Honey comes with its own floral accent, something that works wonderfully paired with soy sauce, which is perhaps why they are so often used together.

**DARK BROWN SUGAR** is considered nourishing in Chinese culture. It's often used as the sweetener for postpartum recovery sweet soups. Some Asian markets stock packs of brown sugar labeled specifically as postpartum brown sugar, but it's just regular brown sugar.

**GRANULATED SUGAR** is perfectly acceptable to use.

**MAPLE SYRUP** is one of my favorite sweeteners for sauces since it's a liquid. It has deep caramel accents.

**COARSE RAW SUGAR** is a light golden color, and coarser-grained than granulated white sugar. I love its intrinsic subtle notes of molasses and caramel.

**ROCK SUGAR** (冰糖 *bīng táng*) can be broken up with a mortar and pestle; it is great in braises and sauces since it contributes a bit more syrupy texture when dissolved.

**HOISIN SAUCE** is a thick, sweet, slightly salty condiment. I love the sweetness and depth it adds to a salty broth. Use it in stir-fries or as a dipping sauce.

**CARAMELIZED ONIONS OR SHALLOTS** are each transformed from a piquant, sharp raw allium to something buttery and sweet. Don't discount these as sources of sweetener. See **Miso-Braised Eggs with Shallots (page 138)**.

**JAMS** are not just for spreading over toast. They can provide sweetness as well as fruity notes that can prevent your sauces from being monotone. See **Sweet and Sour Mushrooms (page 171)**.

—

# 酸 suān (sour)

## VINEGARS • LEMONS • PICKLED THINGS • TAMARIND

**VINEGARS** There are so many to choose from! In addition to the ones below, it's a good idea to have varieties like red wine vinegar and balsamic vinegar in your pantry to bring other accents to your cooking. The complexity and tang of vinegar will change depending on whether you're using a splash of it just as is, in a vinaigrette with oil, or subjecting it to heat as in a braise or stir-fry.

• **Black vinegar** (镇江香醋 zhèn jiāng xiāng cù)

is also called Chinkiang vinegar (the Cantonese romanization of 镇江 Zhenjiang, the city in the Jiangsu province where it comes from). It's a fermented, aged rice vinegar that is full bodied, fragrant, malty, and mildly sweet. It not only makes a great dipping vinegar but also is stunning in brines for pickling, in sauces, and for layering into cooking. In fact, the Chinese name literally translates to fragrant vinegar, not black vinegar.
• **Rice vinegar** (白米醋 bái mǐ cù) is another type of vinegar, sweeter and mellower than black

vinegar, with subtle fruity notes that make it great for a mild pickle.

**LEMONS** are like flaky salt: excellent for that finishing touch. You can use every bit of it: the floral zest, the acidic juice, the pulpy tangy-sweet flesh.

• **Preserved lemons:** New York Shuk has a lovely preserved lemon paste that you can buy online. It's particularly helpful if you aren't in the practice of making preserved whole lemons at home.

**PICKLED THINGS** like pickled onions or kimchi can add acidity, crunch, and sweetness to a dish. Use that pickle brine!

**TAMARIND** comes from the pulp of tamarind tree pods, and is available as a concentrate or puree. It brings floral and fruity accents, in addition to sour.

# 麻 má (numbing)

## RED SICHUAN PEPPERCORNS • GREEN SICHUAN PEPPERCORNS

**RED SICHUAN PEPPERCORNS** (花椒 *huā jiāo*) lend both heat and numbing flavor. They are one of the workhorse spices I use frequently in my cooking. I have a small cast-iron spice grinder (**see page 24**) in which I coarsely grind the whole peppercorns to sprinkle in when I'm cooking.

**GREEN SICHUAN PEPPERCORNS** (青花椒 *qīng huā jiāo*) are more mouth-numbing than the red, and have more citrusy undertones. If you're looking for more of that mala (numbing and spicy) quality and want less heat, use these.

# 辣 là (spicy)

## RED PEPPER FLAKES • GOCHUJANG • DRIED CHILE PEPPERS
## FRESH CHILE PEPPERS • CHILE CRISP • CHILE PASTES • BLACK
## PEPPERCORNS • WHITE PEPPERCORNS • HOT AND SMOKED PAPRIKA

**RED PEPPER FLAKES** can contribute heat at any point in the cooking process. You can also make your own red pepper flakes by pulsing dried whole chile peppers.

• **Gochugaru** (Korean red pepper flakes) is excellent to keep on hand. It's sweet, fragrant, and mildly spicy.

**GOCHUJANG** (Korean fermented chile paste) has sweet and floral undertones like gochugaru but is more concentrated. In addition to heat and fragrance, it has umami from the fermentation process. Use it carefully—gochujang can dominate the flavors in a dish.

**DRIED CHILE PEPPERS,** such as Sichuan 二荆条, *èr jīng tiáo,* can add a lot of heat and flavor. Toasting or blooming in oil will activate the flavors.

**FRESH CHILE PEPPERS** such as Thai chiles, jalapeños, habaneros, and serranos contribute heat and fragrance in a different way from their dried counterparts. Remember: much of the spicy oil lives in the seeds, so if you want a milder heat, remove them before using the chile.

**CHILE CRISP,** like my **Fried Shallot Chile Crisp (page 207)** or commercially available ones such as Lao Gan Ma or Fly By Jing, gives a punch of flavor as well as contributing crispy bits that can add another flavor or textural layer to a dish. Be careful, though—too much and it can quickly become the dominant flavor.

**CHILE PASTES** like sambal oelek, harissa, and sriracha have varying flavor profiles, with some more garlicky (sriracha) and some more smoky (harissa). It might be a bit excessive, but I love having all of these on hand, depending on

what overall flavor profile I am going for and how I'm using it for balance. Can you tell I love spicy heat?

**BLACK PEPPERCORNS** should always be freshly ground, since grinding releases their aroma, making them more fragrant than preground black pepper can ever be. These peppercorns contain piperine that is perceived as hot or spicy, which explains why we feel that zing. Black and white peppercorns are different states of a fruit from the same plant. Black peppercorns are processed with the skin, whereas white peppercorns are soaked to remove the skin. So black peppercorns have a bit more floral flavor, while white peppercorns have a more funky, fermented flavor. Use at every step: prepping, cooking, serving—a perfect pairing with salt.

**WHITE PEPPERCORNS** (白胡椒 *bái hú jiāo*) are available whole or ground into a fine powder. In contrast to black pepper, which should always be freshly ground, I recommend using preground white pepper powder, since it's often used as a final accent, and the fine powder disperses immediately to impart its spicy flavor.

**HOT PAPRIKA** and **SMOKED PAPRIKA** have a deep, complex heat that I'm enamored with. Smoked paprika adds that extra accent of char. I use both frequently.

—

# 苦 kǔ (bitter)

Although this flavor is usually viewed unfavorably, the intrinsic bitterness of a food can add complexity when properly balanced. Radicchio, broccoli rabe, and bitter melon are examples of vegetables with a bite that can be transformed into a positive bitterness when tempered with other flavor elements, such as sweetness—see **Garlicky Radicchio and Pork Stir-Fry, page 80.**

# 香 xiāng (aromatic)

**SESAME • WINES • FIVE-SPICE POWDER • FRESH HERBS
DRIED SPICES • AROMATICS**

## SESAME

• **Toasted sesame oil** has a strong fragrance from pressed toasted sesame seeds. It's best added at the end for a finishing touch. Try to look for pure toasted sesame oil, and start drizzling just a little bit into everything. Yun Hai Taiwanese Pantry has a lovely toasted sesame oil. I also like the Kadoya brand.

• **Sesame paste** is made from toasted sesame seeds, and has a strong sesame flavor—perfect in sauces or dressings.

• **Tahini paste** is made from untoasted sesame seeds and tends to be more mild and a bit bitter. It's also great in sauces or dressings.

• **Toasted sesame seeds** can be a great garnish for anything, and are wonderful for coating flatbreads.

## WINES

• **Shaoxing wine** (绍兴黄酒 *shào xīng huáng jiǔ*) is a yellow rice wine with a deep amber hue and an amazingly deep, fragrant flavor. If you make **Wine-Braised Duck Legs with Beans (page 141)** or **Dōng Pō Ròu (page 133),** you'll see how Shaoxing wine can star in a meal. A little splash of it can bring immediate fragrance to a stir-fry—try it when stir-frying greens (**Light-Fried Leafy Greens, page 71).**

• **High-proof Chinese white liquor** (白酒 *bái jiǔ*) is often passed around in little cups for celebrations or gatherings, but can also be used in fermentation to prevent bad bacterial growth. You can find it in Chinese groceries, and I've seen it sold in the liquor section at Whole Foods. But

in a pinch, you can use vodka, which is similarly high-proof.

• **Mirin** is a milder but still great substitute for Shaoxing wine. It is a sweetened wine, so be aware of this when using.

**FIVE-SPICE POWDER** (五香粉 *wǔ xiāng fěn*) is made of ground red Sichuan peppercorns, cassia (cinnamon), star anise, fennel seeds, and cloves. It's an easy, aromatic spice mix to add to anything.

**FRESH HERBS** such as parsley, cilantro, tarragon, dill, and sage, to name a few favorites, can add freshness and fragrance to a dish. Throw a handful of torn fresh herbs over your dish and see how it can brighten things up.

**DRIED SPICES** I will leave these up to you. There are so many that are considered essential, depending on individual preferences. My favorite spice shop is Curio Spice, in Boston. I pared down my dried spice shelf significantly so that I can buy high-quality ones in small amounts on a regular basis. Poor-quality spices or spices with an expired date are like dust, contributing minimally to your cooking.

**AROMATICS**, particularly **SCALLIONS** (葱 *cōng*), **GINGER** (姜 *jiāng*), and **GARLIC** (蒜 *suàn*), are the holy trinity in Chinese cooking. A quick blooming of these aromatics in hot oil can kick off a dish. See illustrations on **preparing ginger, garlic, and scallion (page 28).**

# MY GO-TO KITCHEN TOOLS

Kitchen equipment is very specific to the individual. The knife that I prefer may not be suitable for your hands. The wok I love is made of carbon steel and therefore admittedly higher maintenance, and may not suit your needs. The beauty of cooking at home is that you can curate your own tools.

**BAMBOO STEAMER BASKET** For steaming dumplings, vegetables, egg, and fish, the steamer gets a lot of mileage in my kitchen. **See page 35** for more information on how to use one.

**WOK** The quintessential pan when it comes to Chinese cuisine. It's deep, with sloped slides, making it masterful at retaining heat and perfect for the dancing rhythm of a stir-fry. Its shape also makes it conducive to deep-frying (a **candy thermometer** will be handy here), braising, and steaming. My preferred wok is made of carbon steel, and it has a rounded bottom that sits on a wok ring on my gas stove. I prefer carbon steel for the following reasons: it is light, quickly responds to heat, heats evenly, and becomes fairly nonstick with proper care (see below). Flat-bottomed woks are available, but I like a round bottom, or a minimally flat bottom, so I can use the curve to scoop and toss ingredients and promote movement and circulation. A wok ring helps your round-bottomed wok sit sturdily on your burner—traditionally, there will be a scoop directly on the range to fit a round-bottomed wok, but we work with what we have. A well-cared-for seasoned carbon-steel wok is a powerhouse on the stove and can last a long time. Woks are also sold in cast iron, stainless steel, and nonstick (though I don't recommend this, as wok cooking potential is unlocked with higher heat, and a nonstick coating cannot handle this). I also recommend a **wok spatula,** which is essential for moving around the contents of your stir-fry and for scraping up food along the bottom of the pan. A **wok lid** will help when you're steaming or simmering food. When I purchased my wok in Shanghai, it came with a cedar wood lid that imparts an additional fragrance, but any lid that fits will suffice.

**HOW TO SEASON YOUR CARBON-STEEL WOK** To protect your wok, you have to season it, which means adding a very thin protective film of oil on the surface. This will maintain

your wok and improve its performance by giving it a nonstick quality.

**FOR THE FIRST USE** Scrub the wok out with hot, soapy water, and dry thoroughly. I like to place it on a burner over low heat until all the water has evaporated. Then start the seasoning process: Over high heat, heat the wok until it is smoking. Rotate the wok and tip it back and forth to ensure every inch is exposed to the heat. The color will change and indicate its progress. Then turn the heat to low and add about one tablespoon of cooking oil. Swirl it around to reach as much of the surface as you can. Turn the heat off, then with long cooking chopsticks or a long pair of tongs, use a thin slice of ginger or a 2-inch piece of scallion to rub that oil all over the inside surface of the wok.

**FOR MAINTENANCE** After every use, rinse, wiping with a soft sponge (with soap if you need to); dry completely over lower heat; then rub canola oil onto the inside surface with a towel. **Do not let your wok soak**.

**OTHER POTS AND PANS** for all your cooking needs, such as:
• **Stockpot** to make stock, ideally large enough to fit a whole chicken
• **Saucepan** large enough to fit in dried long pasta or a bunch of greens for blanching
• **Small saucepan with a pour spout** to heat fats for sizzling
• **10- to 12-inch nonstick skillet** for searing and pan-frying, ideally with a lid
• **Dutch oven** with a wide base and heavy bottom, usable both on the stovetop and in the oven. I'm partial to enamel-coated cast iron such as Staub cocottes, and to a **clay pot**, which is excellent at retaining and circulating heat (ideal for braising) and also doubles as a gorgeous serving dish.

**COOKING CHOPSTICKS** are an absolute must-have! They're different from eating chop-sticks in their length—ideal for reaching into pots while distancing you from heat. I even bring my trusty pair with me to Airbnbs when I know I'll be cooking. They're wooden, beat up, and singed and charred in some places, and I treasure them more than I do any other cooking utensil. They're the perfect tool for tasting as I cook.

**KNIVES** are critical and very individual to suit your hands and grip. I'm partial to my **vegetable cleaver** (this is different from a meat cleaver, which is heavier and meant to chop through bone). It chops, slices, and minces, and it can also smush and crush with the flat side of the blade. Use it with a solid wooden **cutting board** that is still maneuverable enough to pick up and sweep ingredients directly into a pot.

**BOX GRATERS** and **MICROPLANE ZESTERS** can unleash the fragrance of citrus by grating or shredding the zest. And you can use them for so much more. I love my box grater because I can also use it to shred potatoes and grate cheese.

Use a **BLENDER** to make **Ginger-Scallion Water (page 252)** [pork and shrimp wontons in Wrap]—trust me, this infused water will make a world of difference in your bao, dumpling, and wonton fillings, contributing aromatics without compromising texture. I always make an extra batch of the infused water, which I can then throw into sauces or stir-fries in lieu of plain water.

A **CAST-IRON SPICE GRINDER** is a bit of a specialty tool, but one I have grown to rely on almost daily. It's replaced my mortar and pestle for crushing spices or sesame seeds. Mine is made by Zassenhaus. It's heavy and can easily crush whole peppercorns.

**HALF SHEET BAKING PANS** that fit in your oven and freezer can be used not only to bake things in, but also to hold rows of neatly wrapped wontons for freezing.

# COMMON CHOPPING TECHNIQUES

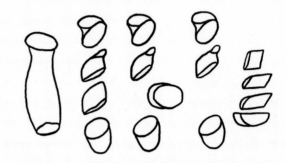

滚刀 **GǓN DĀO,** or "rolled-knife" oblique cutting: a way to obtain an irregular polyhedron without any parallel facing planes. This is used specifically with cylindrical vegetables. A first cut is made on an angle, then the vegetable is rolled about a third of the way and a second bias cut is made. It's then rolled another third of the way and cut again on the bias to form another piece. This maximizes surface area, and is great in braising or soups.

切菱形 **QIĒ LÍNG XÍNG:** slice into a rhombus or parallelogram. Start by cutting the cylindrical food into segments on an angle. Lay the angled piece on a cut side, then slice thin.

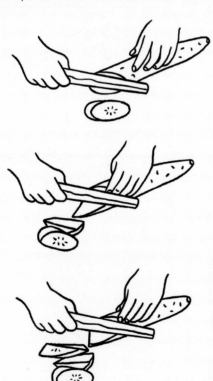

切丝 **QIĒ SĪ,** 切条, **QIĒ TIÁO:** julienne, cut into matchsticks, shred, sliver. After slicing thin, lay the slices flat on the cut side and then cut length-wise into thin strips. The difference between sī and tiáo is thickness, with tiáo being thicker than sī.

切片 **QIĒ PIÀN:** slice thin

**切丁 QIĒ DĪNG, 切米 QIĒ MǏ:** dice; dīng is larger than mǐ. First slice into matchsticks, then cut crosswise to dice.

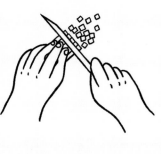

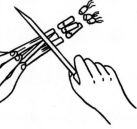

**斜切 XIÉ QIĒ:** slice on a bias, with the knife at a 30-degree angle to the vegetable

**切碎 QIĒ SUÌ:** loose-mince, typically referring to herbs such as cilantro or scallion; loose means not mashed. To loose-mince, slice thin first, as in 切花 QIĒ

**切段 QIĒ DUÀN:** cut into sections or batons, as with scallions

# GARLIC

### 1. SMASH
压 yā

**切末 QIĒ MÒ:** fine-mince, to the point of almost mashing, as with a garlic clove or hand-minced meat. You use a Microplane zester to do this with garlic.

### 2. SLICE
切片 qiē piàn

**切花 QIĒ HUĀ:** finely slice crosswise for garnishes, such as scallions

### 3. MINCE
切末 qiē mò

# SCALLION

# GINGER

### 1. CUT INTO SECTIONS
切段 *qiē duàn*

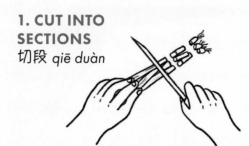

### 1. PEEL
去皮 *qù pí*

### 2. SLIVER/SHRED
切丝 *qiē sī*, then place in cold water to make curls

### 2. SLICE
切片 *qiē piàn*

### 3. CHOP
切花 *qiē huā*

### 3. JULIENNE
切条 *qiē tiáo*

### 4. CUT AT AN ANGLE
斜切 *xié qiē*

### 4. MINCE
切末 *qiē mò*

### 5. MINCE
切碎 *qiē suì*

### 5. GRATE
磨碎 *mó suì*

# RECIPE GUIDE

## 蒸

*zhēng*

# STEAM

剁椒鱼豆腐  Steamed Whole Fish with Tofu | 39

蒜蓉蒸丝瓜  Garlicky Steamed Sponge Gourd | 40

双色馒头  Two-Color Steamed Sweet Potato Buns | 43

———

Buttery Steamed Broccolini with Fish Sauce | 44

Tomato-Bacon Sticky Rice | 47

Dashi-Steamed Mushrooms | 48

Carrots with Mala Pepitas | 51

Steamed Sweet Potatoes with Lemon-Gochujang Butter | 52

Steamed Eggplant with Tamarind Vinaigrette | 55

Glass Noodles with Charred Leeks and Soft Tofu | 56

Rice with Tinned Fish and Dill | 59

Cod with Black Garlic Butter | 60

Miso-Sesame Chicken with Pearl Barley | 63

Hojicha Brown Sugar Prosperity Cakes (Fā Gāo) | 64

Steaming is a healthy, simple, and fast method to cook food that shows off its intrinsic flavors. It does not equal bland or mushy. In this chapter, I'll show you that steaming is a foundational cooking technique, that you can do it with minimal fuss, and that it can involve big flavors.

You've probably already encountered steaming in some way, as it can happen without the classic setup of a steamer. Do you bake bread in a covered Dutch oven? Cook clams in a large pot, lid on, with just an inch of water? Bake fish wrapped in parchment paper? Well, then you've steamed!

Traditional steaming involves placing food over briskly simmering water, usually on a perforated surface, with the lid on. As water becomes gas during evaporation, the cloud of steam rises and encases the food. Despite being as hot as boiling water, steam is a gentle, uniform way to deliver heat because its blanket of minuscule water droplets is less dense—and thus less intense—than liquid.

Steaming is a highly versatile technique. You can flavor the food at any point in the process.

You can do so at the outset, by marinating the food before adding it to the steamer. You can do it during the steaming, either by adding flavoring ingredients to the heatproof dish in which the food cooks, or by steaming the ingredient partially submerged in a savory liquid such as dashi. Or you can flavor after steaming, with a quick sauce. You can even combine steaming with other cooking techniques. For instance, you can start by steaming and then fry if you crave a brown, crispy result—this method works well with potatoes. An initial steaming gives eggplant a creamy texture, after which you can braise it in a rich liquid flavored with gochujang (**see page 142**).

There are several things to keep in mind when you steam. Be careful not to burn yourself when you lift the lid of your steamer, because steam is *very* hot. Check the water regularly and replenish it so you don't burn your pot or bamboo steamer. And since this method of cooking depends on circulation, make sure you leave space around the food so the steam can do its work.

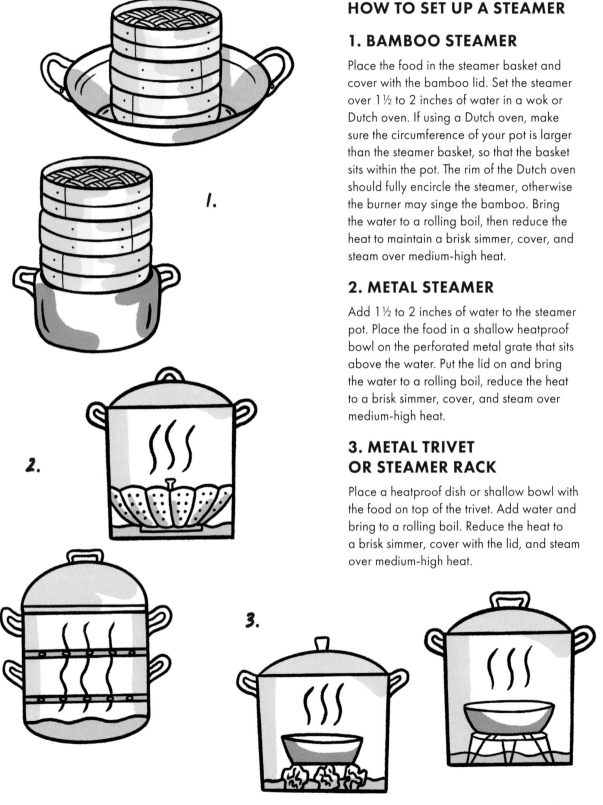

## HOW TO SET UP A STEAMER

### 1. BAMBOO STEAMER

Place the food in the steamer basket and cover with the bamboo lid. Set the steamer over 1 ½ to 2 inches of water in a wok or Dutch oven. If using a Dutch oven, make sure the circumference of your pot is larger than the steamer basket, so that the basket sits within the pot. The rim of the Dutch oven should fully encircle the steamer, otherwise the burner may singe the bamboo. Bring the water to a rolling boil, then reduce the heat to maintain a brisk simmer, cover, and steam over medium-high heat.

### 2. METAL STEAMER

Add 1 ½ to 2 inches of water to the steamer pot. Place the food in a shallow heatproof bowl on the perforated metal grate that sits above the water. Put the lid on and bring the water to a rolling boil, reduce the heat to a brisk simmer, cover, and steam over medium-high heat.

### 3. METAL TRIVET OR STEAMER RACK

Place a heatproof dish or shallow bowl with the food on top of the trivet. Add water and bring to a rolling boil. Reduce the heat to a brisk simmer, cover with the lid, and steam over medium-high heat.

## EQUIPMENT

All you need is a wok or a deep pot, a heat-friendly vessel that fits in the pot and something to raise it above the water level, and a lid for the pot to trap all that lovely steam. I prefer bamboo steamers because they stack, and they impart a beautiful fragrance to food. Equally important, the bamboo lid absorbs condensation, so you don't have to worry about drops of water diluting the flavors. (If you use a stainless-steel steamer or other pot, wrap a cloth around the lid to absorb those water droplets.) You can also steam in a dedicated metal steamer pot, on a metal trivet, or in a steamer cage or basket. Clever do-it-yourself setups to elevate the food above the water include an upside-down heatproof bowl, an upside-down aluminum pie plate with a bunch of holes poked in the bottom, or even balls of aluminum foil.

## HOW TO SET UP A STEAMER

Any heatproof dish you use to hold the food should fit within your steamer with at least ½ inch to spare to allow for the circulation of steam. If the food you are steaming doesn't need a dish (such as buns), you can line your steamer basket with parchment paper with holes cut into it.

If using a bamboo steamer, ensure that the lid fits securely; if using a trivet, make sure the lid to the pot will close over the setup. Cover the basket or pot. Maintain enough heat for a brisk simmer, and replenish the water when necessary. I go by audible cues and listen for gentle bubbling.

# APPROXIMATE STEAMING TIMES FOR SOME COMMON VEGETABLES

These are average times. Remember the timing will vary with the size of the vegetables or slices.

**ASPARAGUS**
6 to 7 minutes

**BROCCOLI**
5 to 7 minutes

**CABBAGE**
5 to 7 minutes

**CARROTS**
8 to 10 minutes

**CAULIFLOWER**
6 to 7 minutes

**CORN ON THE COB**
8 minutes

**EGGPLANT**
5 to 8 minutes

**GREEN BEANS**
4 to 5 minutes

**KABOCHA SQUASH**
10 to 20 minutes

**LEAFY VEGETABLES**
3 minutes

**ROOT VEGETABLES**
8 to 10 minutes

**STARCHY ROOTS (POTATO)**
10 to 12 minutes

**SWEET POTATO AND YAM**
20 to 25 minutes

# STEAMED WHOLE FISH WITH TOFU

剁椒鱼豆腐 | *duò jiāo yú dòu fu* | Serves 4

To all those folks who equate steaming with bland, I respond with this dish. Sharp, tangy, and hot, 剁椒, *duò jiāo*, are salted and pickled chopped chile peppers from the Hunan Province. Their spicy flavor permeates the flesh of the fish and tofu so you don't need any additional flavoring. Traditionally this dish is made with a large fish head, but I like to use a whole fish, such as a sea bass or snapper.

1. Cut two or three slits 2 to 2½ inches long into each side of the fish, three-quarters of the way through the flesh, not reaching the bone. Combine the salt and 1 teaspoon of the sugar. Sprinkle and rub it over the fish, including the interior and in the slits. Let cure for 30 minutes in the refrigerator.

2. Add the oil to a wok or large skillet over medium-high heat. Add the ginger and garlic and fry until fragrant, about 30 seconds. Add the salted chile peppers and fermented black beans (if using), and stir-fry until fragrant and softened, 1 to 2 minutes.

3. Mix together the soy sauce and the remaining 1 tablespoon sugar, then add to the wok. Let the mixture bubble briefly, then remove from the heat. If you're going to use a wok–bamboo steamer setup, scrape the chile mixture into a small bowl and clean out the wok.

4. Rinse the fish thoroughly and pat dry. Brush with the Shaoxing wine.

5. Cut the tofu in half lengthwise, then slice into ½-inch squares. Arrange the tofu around the edges of a shallow heatproof bowl that will fit into your steamer.

6. Place the fish on top of the tofu, nestling it in the center. Set a bamboo steamer over 2 inches of water in the wok or add 2 inches of water to a metal steamer pot and place the steamer basket in the pot. Bring to a boil, then reduce the heat to a brisk simmer. Place the bowl with the tofu and fish in the steamer, cover, and steam over medium-high heat for 4 minutes.

7. Carefully remove the bowl from the steamer, pour off the liquid, and spoon the chile pepper sauce over the fish.

8. Return the bowl to the steamer, cover, and steam for an additional 5 minutes or until the fish flakes easily with a fork.

9. Top with the scallions and serve immediately.

1 whole fish (1 to 1½ pounds/455 g to 680 g) such as striped bass, scaled and gutted, head and tail left on

2 teaspoons kosher salt

1 tablespoon plus 1 teaspoon sugar, divided

2 tablespoons neutral oil, such as canola or grapeseed

3 garlic cloves, minced

1 tablespoon minced peeled ginger

¼ cup duò jiāo (Hunan salted chopped chile peppers), drained

1 teaspoon douchi (fermented black beans; optional)

2 tablespoons light soy sauce

1 tablespoon Shaoxing wine

1 pound (455 g) soft tofu

2 scallions, trimmed and minced

**SUBSTITUTE:** You can also do this recipe with 4 fillets.

# GARLICKY STEAMED SPONGE GOURD

蒜蓉蒸丝瓜 | *suàn róng zhēng sī guā* | Serves 4

**The sponge gourd,** 丝瓜 *sī guā,* **is an underrated Asian vegetable. It's delightful in a stir-fry, where it's often paired with tofu puffs, but it is steaming that allows its juicy texture to shine. Steaming also lends it a lighter feel, without the oil of frying, so it's a refreshing dish in the summer. This simple, winning technique can be applied to most vegetables.**

One 21-ounce (600 g) sponge gourd

3 tablespoons neutral oil, such as canola or grapeseed

5 garlic cloves, minced

2 red Thai chile peppers, stemmed and roughly chopped

2 tablespoons light soy sauce

1 tablespoon Shaoxing wine

1 teaspoon sugar

¼ teaspoon ground white pepper

1. Slice off the base and stem end of the gourd and discard. Slice the remaining gourd crosswise into ½-inch-thick rounds.

2. Heat the oil in a wok or large skillet over medium-high heat. Add the garlic and chile peppers and cook until fragrant. (Beware the steam from the chiles, which can irritate your eyes.)

3. Remove from the heat and stir in the soy sauce, Shaoxing wine, sugar, and white pepper. If you're going to use a wok–bamboo steamer setup, pour into a small bowl and clean out the wok.

4. Place the sponge gourd rounds in a single layer on a heatproof plate that will fit into your steamer. Set a bamboo steamer over 2 inches of water in the wok or add 2 inches of water to a metal steamer pot and place the steamer basket in the pot. Bring to a boil. Place the plate in the steamer, cover, and steam over medium-high heat for 7 minutes or until the sponge gourd is tender all the way through.

5. Remove from the steamer and transfer to a serving platter. Drizzle the chile-garlic sauce over the sponge gourd and serve immediately.

**NOTE:** For a complete meal, add 2 or 3 bundles of glass noodles (2½ to 3½ ounces/75 to 100 g each) as a bed for the sponge gourd rounds. Soak the noodles in hot water for 2 to 3 minutes, until soft, then drain well. Transfer to the heatproof plate, add the sponge gourd, and steam as directed.

**SUBSTITUTES:** If you can't find sponge gourd, you can substitute Chinese broccoli, 芥蓝 *gài lán; choy sum,* 菜心 *cài xīn;* or another green.

# TWO-COLOR STEAMED SWEET POTATO BUNS

双色馒头 | *shuāng sè mán tou* | Makes 8 buns

**Steamed buns called *mantou* are a staple in northern China where bread and noodles are more ubiquitous than rice. All over China, you will see daily commuters on the move carrying thin plastic bags holding their mantou. They are a delicious breakfast on the go. Or serve them as a great vehicle to mop up a soup or braise. The two-toned pinwheel appearance of these steamed buns comes from layering separate doughs, one tinted orange by sweet potato, the other plain. The doughs are stacked, rolled into a log, then sliced.**

1. Cut eight 3-inch squares of parchment paper and set aside.

2. Peel the sweet potato and cut it into 1- to 2-inch-thick slices. Steam over high heat until soft, approximately 20 minutes. Set the sweet potato aside until cool, then mash with a fork until smooth. Measure out ¼ cup (70 g) and set aside.

3. Lightly oil two large bowls. Divide the bao dough in half. Form one half into a ball and knead for 7 to 8 minutes, until the dough is soft, elastic, and smooth. Place the dough in one of the oiled bowls. Cover with plastic wrap.

4. Knead the mashed sweet potato into the other half of the dough, along with the flour, 1 teaspoon oil, and the sugar. Knead for 5 minutes or until the sweet potato is thoroughly incorporated. If the dough becomes too wet (depending on your sweet potato), add more flour 1 table-spoon at a time until the dough is soft, elastic, and smooth. Continue kneading until the dough doesn't stick to your hands. If you stretch it, it should offer some resistance and pull back. Place the sweet potato dough in the other bowl and cover with plastic wrap.

5. Let both doughs rise for 45 to 60 minutes, until they are 1½ times their original size. Roll out each dough into about a 10 by 12-inch rectangle, about ¼-inch thick.

6. Brush the sweet potato dough lightly with water, then lay the plain dough over it. Gently roll the stacked doughs with a rolling pin to meld the two layers. Roll the dough up, starting from the long edge. Cut the log crosswise into eight pieces and lay each on a parchment square.

7. Cover with plastic wrap and let rise for 15 minutes in a warm, draft-free place (like an oven heated to the lowest setting and turned off).

8. Set a bamboo steamer over 2 inches of water in a wok or add 2 inches of water to a metal steamer pot and place the steamer basket in the pot. Bring to a brisk simmer over medium-high heat. Working in batches as necessary, place the buns, on their parchment squares, in the steamer and steam over medium-high heat for 12 minutes. The buns should be smooth and bouncy; if you press into one, it should recoil and leave no indent. Serve hot.

1 small sweet potato (10.5 ounces/300 g)

1 teaspoon neutral oil, such as canola or grapeseed, plus more for the bowls

**Bao Dough (page 254)**

½ cup (63 g) all-purpose flour, plus more as needed

2 tablespoons sugar

**NOTE:** These buns freeze wonderfully for up to 2 months. After steaming, let cool, then place them in rows on a baking sheet lined with parchment paper and freeze. Once frozen, you can place them in a freezer-safe container. To reheat, simply steam for 5 minutes, or microwave for 2 minutes with a damp paper towel (to prevent drying out).

# BUTTERY STEAMED BROCCOLINI WITH FISH SAUCE

Serves 2

**The broccoli family is a great candidate for steaming, which coaxes out the natural sweetness of the stems while retaining their crunch. I love broccolini because it's more delicate than a regular broccoli head, making it very quick to steam. Here, I bathe it in a fish sauce–infused butter and flavor-steam the whole thing. The dish is my take on the classic 芥蓝 *gài lán* (Chinese broccoli) with oyster sauce, a favorite at dim sum parlors.**

2 tablespoons unsalted butter

1 tablespoon sugar

1 tablespoon freshly squeezed lemon juice

2 teaspoons fish sauce

¼ teaspoon light soy sauce

1 bunch broccolini (7 ounces/200 g), ends trimmed, thicker stalks halved lengthwise

Flaky salt and freshly ground black pepper

1. Melt the butter in a small saucepan over medium heat. When it starts to foam, remove from the heat and stir in the sugar, lemon juice, fish sauce, and soy sauce.

2. Place the broccolini in a single layer on a heatproof plate that will fit into your steamer. Set a bamboo steamer over 2 inches of water in a wok or add 2 inches of water to a metal steamer pot and place the steamer basket in the pot. Bring to a boil, then reduce the heat to a brisk simmer.

3. Pour the butter mixture over the broccolini and place the plate in the steamer. Cover and steam over medium-high heat until crisp-tender, about 4 minutes.

4. Top with the flaky salt and freshly ground black pepper and serve.

**SUBSTITUTE:** You can also use broccoli rabe (steam for 3 minutes), gai lan (4 minutes), or broccoli florets (6 minutes).

# TOMATO-BACON STICKY RICE

Serves 4

**Sticky rice, aka sweet glutinous rice, is best steamed, so its plump, chewy grains are ready to sponge up all the flavor. The dish is a riff on lo mai gai, a dim sum classic. I created it almost by accident when I was obsessed with tomato paste and the umami it can contribute. The result is reminiscent of paella, but with the classic sticky-chewy texture of sweet glutinous rice. You'll end up with a bit of crispy browned rice at the bottom of the pan—scrape it up and fold it into the final mix and savor those crispy bits.**

1. Rinse and drain the sticky rice. Place rice in a shallow heatproof bowl that will fit into your steamer. Steam in two batches if needed.

2. Mix the soy sauce with 1 tablespoon of the tomato paste in a small bowl. Toss with the sticky rice until evenly mixed.

3. Set a bamboo steamer over 2 inches of water. Bring to a boil, then reduce the heat to a brisk simmer.

4. Place the bowl in the steamer, cover, and steam over medium-high heat for 15 minutes or until the rice is translucent and sticky. (It won't be cooked all the way through.)

5. Meanwhile, place the bacon in a single layer in a large nonstick or well-seasoned cast-iron skillet. Set the skillet over medium heat and cook, turning occasionally, until the bacon is crispy and the fat has rendered, 7 to 9 minutes. Remove the bacon and drain on a paper towel–lined plate. When it is cool enough to handle, chop it into ½-inch pieces and set aside.

6. Pour out all but 2 tablespoons of the bacon fat, keeping 1 tablespoon in reserve. Heat over medium-low heat. Add the fennel seeds, smoked paprika, and red pepper flakes and cook until fragrant, about 1 minute. Add the mushrooms and cook undisturbed for 5 to 7 minutes, until browned.

7. If the pan is dry, add the reserved tablespoon bacon fat. Add the white parts of the scallion and the garlic and cook for another 1 to 2 minutes, until softened. Add the remaining 2 teaspoons tomato paste and let caramelize, about 5 minutes.

8. Reduce the heat to low, then add 1 cup of the stock, the sugar, and the salt and stir to combine, scraping up the browned bits from the bottom of the pot. Add the steamed sticky rice and toss to combine, stirring gently and continuously until all the stock is absorbed, 4 to 5 minutes.

9. Add the remaining ½ cup stock and the reserved bacon and mix to combine. Cover and steam for another 5 to 8 minutes, until the rice is fully cooked, sticky, and plump.

10. Fold in the green parts of the scallions, top with lemon zest, and add a squeeze of lemon and serve immediately.

2 cups (460 g) glutinous rice, such as sweet rice or sticky rice, soaked in water overnight

1 tablespoon light soy sauce

2 tablespoons plus 2 teaspoons tomato paste, divided

8 ounces (225 g) thick-cut applewood-smoked bacon

1 teaspoon fennel seeds

1 teaspoon smoked paprika

Pinch of red pepper flakes

5 ounces (140 g) shiitake mushrooms, stemmed and thinly sliced (2 loosely packed cups), or 8 to 10 dried shiitakes rehydrated in hot water for 1 hour, then sliced

3 scallions, trimmed and thinly sliced, white and green parts separated

2 garlic cloves, minced

1½ cups (360 g) unsalted chicken stock, vegetable stock, or water, divided

1 tablespoon sugar

1 teaspoon kosher salt

Zest and juice of 1 lemon

**NOTE:** If using salted stock, omit the kosher salt.

# DASHI-STEAMED MUSHROOMS

Serves 2

**A mix of different mushrooms with a spectrum of shapes and textures are steamed not with water, but by partially submerging them in an umami-packed dashi. In this one-pot method of steaming, the flavorful dashi melds with the natural juices the mushrooms release as they steam, to create a magical broth.**

1 tablespoon neutral oil, such as canola or grapeseed

One ¼-inch-thick piece ginger, julienned

8½ ounces (240 g) mushrooms, preferably a mix **(see Notes)**, cleaned, trimmed, and thinly sliced if large or torn into small clumps

1 cup (240 g) **Dashi (page 195)**

1 tablespoon Shaoxing wine

1 tablespoon light soy sauce

## SMOKY PAPRIKA OIL

2 tablespoons neutral oil, such as canola or grapeseed

½ teaspoon smoked paprika

¼ teaspoon toasted sesame oil

1 scallion, trimmed and sliced on the diagonal into thin ribbons

1. Heat the oil in a medium saucepan with a lid over medium heat. Add the ginger and stir-fry for 30 seconds.

2. Arrange the mushrooms in a single layer in the saucepan. Add the dashi, Shaoxing wine, and soy sauce. The broth should come about one-third of the way up the mushrooms.

3. Bring to a boil, then reduce the heat to the lowest setting, cover, and steam until the mushrooms are tender and have released their liquid, 7 to 9 minutes.

4. **Meanwhile, make the paprika oil:** Heat the neutral oil in a small saucepan over medium heat. When it shimmers, add the smoked paprika. Turn off the heat and stir in the sesame oil.

5. Serve the mushrooms in their broth, drizzled with the paprika oil, with the scallion ribbons on top.

**NOTES:** Shimeji, enoki, shiitake, beech, and wood ear mushrooms are great together—for example, about 1¾ ounces (50 g) beech mushrooms, 1¾ ounces (50 g) shiitake mushrooms, 3½ ounces (100 g) enoki mushrooms, and 1¾ ounces (50 g) wood ear mushrooms.

If you don't have time to make the dashi, you can substitute 1 teaspoon hondashi powder (Japanese dashi seasoning) dissolved in 1 cup hot water.

For a complete meal, add a small fillet of fish, such as salmon, or a delicate white fish like cod. Place the fish over the mushrooms before placing the lid on and steam for an additional 5 minutes, depending on thickness.

# CARROTS WITH MALA PEPITAS

Serves 4

Steaming carrots transforms their flavor and texture. It's a common way to introduce them to babies, because they become soft and sweet. But steamed carrots can also be complex, and they're an excellent foundation on which to build a dish. Pair these with a rich vinaigrette made with some of my favorite ingredients—miso, black vinegar, and maple syrup—and top the carrots with crispy, spicy pepitas, and you get a potent dish with contrasting yet complementary flavors and textures. The pepitas are more than just spicy; they're flavored with a mix of red and green Sichuan peppercorns, a *mala* (mouth-numbing), tingling spice.

1. Place the carrots in a single layer in a steamer basket set inside a medium pot over 2 inches of water. Bring to a boil, then reduce the heat to a brisk simmer, cover, and steam over medium-high heat for 8 to 10 minutes, until fork-tender.

2. Meanwhile, combine the rice vinegar, miso, black vinegar, maple syrup, sesame oil, garlic, and water in a large bowl and set aside.

3. When the carrots are done, immediately toss them with the vinaigrette. Let sit for 5 minutes to absorb the flavors.

4. **Meanwhile, make the mala pepitas:** Heat the neutral oil in a large nonstick skillet over medium heat. Add the pepitas and cook, stirring almost constantly, until they turn golden brown, 3 to 5 minutes. They will sizzle and start to pop as they cook. When they are crispy and golden brown, use a slotted spoon to remove them from the pan and transfer to a bowl. Immediately add the smoked paprika, salt, ground peppercorns, and cayenne and toss the pepitas to coat.

5. Transfer the carrots to a serving dish and top with the spicy pepitas, lemon zest, and chile oil to taste (if using).

1 pound (455 g) medium carrots, trimmed and peeled

1 tablespoon rice vinegar

1 tablespoon white (shiro) miso

1 tablespoon black vinegar

1 tablespoon maple syrup

1 teaspoon toasted sesame oil

2 medium garlic cloves, minced

1 tablespoon water

## MALA PEPITAS

1 tablespoon neutral oil, such as canola or grapeseed

½ cup (80 g) hulled pepitas (pumpkin seeds)

½ teaspoon smoked paprika

½ teaspoon kosher salt

¼ teaspoon ground red Sichuan peppercorns

¼ teaspoon ground green Sichuan peppercorns

¼ teaspoon ground cayenne pepper

Grated zest of 1 lemon

chile oil (optional)

# STEAMED SWEET POTATOES WITH LEMON-GOCHUJANG BUTTER

Serves 4

**Sweet potatoes become fluffy and sweet when steamed, then are flavored with a zingy gochujang butter. The residual heat from the steaming process instantly melts the butter, letting it coat and seep into the sweet potatoes. This simple presentation will wow your dinner guests.**

4 tablespoons (½ stick/115 g) unsalted butter, at room temperature

2 teaspoons maple syrup

1 teaspoon preserved lemon paste or 1 teaspoon minced preserved lemon

1 teaspoon gochujang

2 medium to large sweet potatoes (about 2 pounds/910 g total), scrubbed

Flaky salt and freshly ground black pepper

2 scallions, trimmed and thinly sliced

1. Combine the softened butter, maple syrup, preserved lemon, and gochujang in a small bowl. Let sit for at least 2 hours at room temperature or in the refrigerator to meld the flavors.

2. Cut the sweet potatoes into 1-inch-thick rounds.

3. Set a bamboo steamer over 2 inches of water in a wok or add 2 inches of water to a metal steamer pot and place the steamer basket in the pot. Bring to a boil, then reduce the heat to a brisk simmer. Place a layer of sweet potatoes in the steamer, then pile the remaining pieces on top, allowing space within the "mountain" for steam to circulate. Cover and steam over medium-high heat for 25 to 30 minutes, until the sweet potatoes are easily pierced with a fork.

4. Transfer to a serving plate and immediately dollop the gochujang butter over the sweet potatoes.

5. Sprinkle with flaky salt, pepper, and the scallions. Serve immediately.

# STEAMED EGGPLANT WITH TAMARIND VINAIGRETTE

Serves 4

**Steaming eggplant changes its texture completely. It loses its slippery, fibrous character and becomes creamy and soft, ready to soak up any dressing or sauce it's tossed with. This dressing is made tart and citrusy by tamarind, which is mellowed by maple syrup. I like to tear the eggplant into thin strips by hand to create irregular surfaces, the better to soak up the dressing. A handful of watercress and scallions on top adds a touch of freshness. This dish is best served chilled.**

1. Cut off the base and stem of each eggplant, then cut each one crosswise into 3 pieces. Halve each piece lengthwise, so you have 6 pieces per eggplant.

2. Fill a large bowl with cold water and add the white rice vinegar. Add the eggplant, skin side down, to the water-vinegar mix, and let sit for 10 to 15 minutes. (This step preserves the purple color of the eggplant.)

3. Set a bamboo steamer over 2 inches of water in a wok or add 2 inches of water to the bottom of a metal steamer. Bring to a boil, then reduce the heat to a brisk simmer. Place a layer of eggplant skin side down in the steamer, then pile the remaining pieces on top, allowing space within the "mountain" for steam to circulate. Steam in batches if necessary.

4. Cover and steam over medium-high heat for 5 to 7 minutes, until the eggplant is soft and easily pierced with a chopstick. It should be soft and creamy, but firm enough to hold its shape. Set aside to cool.

5. Meanwhile, combine the garlic, maple syrup, tamarind concentrate, cider vinegar, red pepper flakes, soy sauce, ¼ teaspoon salt, and ¼ teaspoon black pepper in a small bowl. Adjust the sauce to your taste and add more tamarind concentrate if needed.

6. Once the eggplant is cool enough to handle, tear it lengthwise into ¼-inch-thick pieces. Alternatively, you can use a knife to cut into ¼-inch-thick pieces. Arrange on a serving plate and refrigerate until cold, about 30 minutes.

7. Pile the watercress and scallions atop the eggplant. Pour the tamarind dressing over everything and mix gently to combine. Serve.

2 Japanese or Chinese eggplants (12 ounces/340 g total)

2 teaspoons white rice vinegar

2 garlic cloves, minced

2 tablespoons maple syrup

1 tablespoon tamarind concentrate, plus more to taste

1 tablespoon apple cider vinegar

2 teaspoons red pepper flakes

1 teaspoon light soy sauce

Kosher salt and freshly ground black pepper

2 lightly packed cups (45 g) bite-sized pieces watercress

2 scallions, trimmed and sliced on the diagonal into ribbons

# GLASS NOODLES WITH CHARRED LEEKS AND SOFT TOFU

Serves 2 or 3

**Leeks benefit from thorough cooking to bring out their sweet, slightly garlicky flavor. In this recipe, they're incorporated into a slightly sweet, savory sauce, which is soaked up by the tofu and the noodles below. This dish is all about different textures: custardy tofu, crispy leeks, and slippery noodles.**

2 bundles (3½ ounces/100 g each) mung bean noodles or sweet potato noodles

1 large or 2 small leeks (about 12 ounces/340 g total), woody outer layers and root hairs removed, white and pale green parts sliced into thin half-moons

¼ cup (60 g) water

2 tablespoons rice vinegar

2 tablespoons light soy sauce

2 teaspoons honey

2 tablespoons neutral oil, such as canola or grapeseed

1 block (1 pound/455 g) soft or firm tofu

Kosher salt and freshly ground black pepper

2 garlic cloves, minced

1 or 2 small heads bok choy (4 ounces/114 g each), leaves trimmed, separated, and halved lengthwise (optional)

1. Prepare the noodles by soaking them in hot water for 10 minutes or until soft and pliable. Rinse with cold water, drain, and set aside.

2. Meanwhile, in another bowl, cover the sliced leeks with cold water and swish vigorously with your hands to loosen any dirt. Let the dirt settle on the bottom of the bowl, then carefully lift out the leek pieces and drain in a colander.

3. Mix the water, rice vinegar, soy sauce, and honey in a small bowl.

4. Heat the oil in a medium saucepan over medium heat. Add the leeks and sauté until they brown and their edges start to crisp and char, about 7 minutes.

5. Meanwhile, place the noodles in a shallow heatproof bowl that will fit into your steamer. Cut the tofu crosswise into ½-inch-thick slabs. Carefully lay the tofu slabs over the noodles, spreading the pieces out to maximize their exposure to the heat. Sprinkle with salt and pepper.

6. Add the garlic to the saucepan with the leeks and cook for an additional minute, until fragrant. Remove from the heat and let cool for 5 minutes. Pour in the liquid mixture, return the pan to medium heat, and cook until the sauce bubbles and thickens, about 3 minutes.

7. Spoon the leek sauce over the tofu. If using the bok choy, spread it evenly over the tofu on top of the sauce.

8. Set a bamboo steamer over 2 inches of water in a wok or add 2 inches of water to a metal steamer pot and place the steamer basket in the pot. Bring to a boil, then reduce the heat to a brisk simmer. Place the bowl with the noodles and tofu in the steamer.

9. Cover and steam over medium-high heat for 7 to 8 minutes. At this point, the noodles should be slippery and translucent and the tofu heated through. Push the tofu and bok choy (if using) to one side, then mix the noodles well to incorporate all the sauce. Use scissors to cut the noodles, or offer scissors at the table. Serve immediately.

**NOTE:** For the tofu, I prefer soft tofu (don't confuse it with silken tofu), but it may be hard to source outside of Asian stores. If you can't find it, firm will also work.

# RICE WITH TINNED FISH AND DILL

Serves 4

This recipe is one of my favorite ways to pull together a quick, aromatic dinner since I often have tinned sardines or mackerel in my pantry. At first glance, you might not think the recipe belongs in the steamed section, but rice cooked on the stovetop is essentially just another way to steam.

The beauty of this dish is that you can riff on it endlessly, since whatever you add to the rice will impart its fragrance in the steaming process—bok choy does this wonderfully. This one-pot, low-maintenance meal is brightened with fresh lemon juice and aromatic herbs. I generally use a rice cooker. If you don't have one, you can use a clay pot or Dutch oven.

1. Soak the rice in water to cover for 30 minutes, then rinse under running water until the water runs clear.

2. You can cook the rice in a rice cooker, a clay pot, or a small Dutch oven.

   **RICE COOKER METHOD:** Combine the rice and water in the pot of a rice cooker. Stir in the soy sauce, then place the fish in a single layer over the rice. Drizzle the oil from the tin around the edges of the rice—this will help make the rice crispy. Cook on the white rice setting.

   **CLAY POT OR DUTCH OVEN METHOD:** Combine the rice, water, and soy sauce in an 8-inch clay pot or a small Dutch oven. Bring to a boil over medium-high heat. When the water is bubbling, cover tightly and reduce the heat to its lowest setting. Cook for 10 minutes. Uncover and spread the fish in a single layer over the rice. Drizzle the oil from the tin around the edges of the rice—this will make the rice crispy. Cover again and cook, still over the lowest heat, for another 10 minutes. Uncover, increase the heat to medium-high, and cook uncovered for 4 to 5 minutes, until you hear sizzling. Turn off the heat and let stand for another 5 minutes.

3. Uncover the pot and add the dill, lemon zest and juice, and the butter. Mix thoroughly, breaking up the fish. Sprinkle with flaky salt and the pepper, then serve.

1½ cups plus 2 tablespoons (320 g) long-grain white rice

1¼ cups plus 2 tablespoons (330 g) water for a rice cooker, or 2¼ cups (540 g) water for a clay pot or Dutch oven

2 teaspoons light soy sauce

One 4.375-ounce (124 g) tin sardines or mackerel in olive oil

½ packed cup (35 g) roughly chopped fresh dill

Grated zest and juice of 1 lemon

1 tablespoon unsalted butter

Flaky salt and freshly ground black pepper

**NOTE:** You can add 8 ounces/225 g leafy greens, chopped, such as bok choy or napa cabbage, strewing them over the fish. Decrease the water to 1¼ cups (300 g) for a rice cooker, and to 2 cups (475 g) for the clay pot method.

**SUBSTITUTE:** You can use shiso, Chinese celery leaves, or fennel fronds instead of the dill.

# COD WITH BLACK GARLIC BUTTER

Serves 2 to 4

**I turn to steaming whenever I have a delicate white fish such as cod, since the gentle, moist heat prevents it from drying out. I start with a quick dry cure, a mix of sugar and salt. This curing step firms up the fish and subtly seasons it. Then I flavor-steam the cod with the aromatics Shaoxing wine and ginger, after which I sauce it with a sizzling sauce of browned butter and fermented black garlic, which adds notes of caramel sweetness and funk.**

2 teaspoons kosher salt

1 teaspoon sugar

1 pound (455 g) cod or other skinless white fish fillet, 1½ to 2 inches thick, cut into 2 pieces, patted dry

3 black garlic cloves, peeled

1 tablespoon Shaoxing wine

Two ⅛-inch-thick slices ginger

2 scallions, trimmed and minced

3 tablespoons unsalted butter

Flaky salt and freshly ground black pepper

Lemon wedges

1. Combine the salt and sugar in a small bowl. Rub all over the cod and let sit for 15 minutes in the fridge.

2. Meanwhile, crush the black garlic to a smooth paste with a mortar and pestle or with the flat side of your knife. Set aside.

3. Rinse the cod fillets, pat dry, and place in a shallow heatproof bowl that will fit into your steamer. Brush the fillets with the Shaoxing wine and lay a slice of ginger on top of each.

4. Set a bamboo steamer over 2 inches of water in a wok or add 2 inches of water to a metal steamer and place the steamer basket in the pot. Bring to a boil, then reduce the heat to a brisk simmer. Place the bowl with the fillets in the steamer. Cover and steam over medium-high heat for 5 to 8 minutes, until the fish flakes easily. (The exact timing will depend on the thickness of the fish.)

5. Discard the ginger slices, then transfer the fillets to serving plates. Scatter the minced scallions over them.

6. Melt the butter in a small saucepan over medium heat. Add the crushed black garlic and cook until the butter browns, mashing the garlic in the pan with a wooden spoon, 5 to 7 minutes. Pour over the cod.

7. Sprinkle with flaky salt and pepper and serve immediately with lemon wedges for squeezing.

# MISO-SESAME CHICKEN WITH PEARL BARLEY

Serves 4

**This dish is inspired by the restorative classic sesame chicken soup, which is traditionally served to mothers after they give birth. Boneless chicken thighs are marinated in a miso-sesame combination before being steamed, which releases their juices, flavoring a bed of nutty barley below and almost becoming a stew.**

1. **Make the marinade:** Mix all the ingredients in a small bowl. Pour into a resealable plastic bag or container, add the chicken and stir. Let sit in the fridge for at least 2 hours or overnight.

2. Bring a medium saucepan of water to a boil over high heat. Add the barley and cook until al dente, 15 to 20 minutes. Drain and set aside until you're ready to cook the chicken.

3. The chicken should have absorbed much of the marinade—if not, stir a few more times. Fold in the cornstarch slurry.

4. Set a bamboo steamer over 2 inches of water in a wok or add 2 inches of water to a metal steamer and place the steamer basket in the pot. Bring to a boil, then reduce the heat to a brisk simmer.

5. Spread the cooked barley in a large, shallow heatproof bowl that will fit into your steamer. Layer the chicken over the pearl barley. Place the bowl in the steamer, cover, and steam over medium-high heat until the chicken is cooked through—a thermometer should read 165°F. (The wider your bowl, the less time this will take.) Check at 10 minutes; if the chicken is not yet done, stir gently and cook for 5 to 10 minutes more.

6. Remove from the heat, and let sit, still tightly covered, for 5 minutes.

7. **Meanwhile, make the soy-scallion sauce:** Heat the neutral oil in a small saucepan over medium-low heat. Add the scallions and sauté for about 1 minute, until fragrant. Add the water, soy sauce, and sugar, let simmer for another minute until slightly thickened, then remove from the heat.

8. Pour the soy-scallion sauce over the chicken and serve in bowls.

## MISO-SESAME MARINADE

½ cup water

3 tablespoons toasted sesame oil

2 tablespoons red miso

2 tablespoons Shaoxing wine

1 tablespoon light soy sauce

1 tablespoon honey

2 pounds (910 g) boneless, skinless chicken thighs, cut into 1½-inch chunks

½ cup (107 g) medium pearl barley

1 tablespoon cornstarch mixed with 1 tablespoon water

## SOY-SCALLION SAUCE

1 tablespoon neutral oil, such as canola or grapeseed

3 scallions, trimmed and minced

¼ cup (60 g) water

1 tablespoon light soy sauce

1 teaspoon sugar

**SUBSTITUTE:** You can make this dish with bone-in chicken drumsticks or thighs, which are even more succulent. Use a cleaver or heavy knife to chop them into pieces (or ask your butcher to), and add 4 minutes to the cooking time.

# HOJICHA BROWN SUGAR PROSPERITY CAKES (FĀ GĀO)

Makes 8 cakes

Like many other Lunar New Year foods, these steamed yeast-risen cakes are symbolic, setting the tone for the coming year. They're known as prosperity cakes because fā gāo implies making a fortune. How high the batter rises and how open the petals are tell you how lucky your year will be. A thick enough batter, a cross drawn with oil over the surface, and the right container all ensure a good rise.

These cakes are flavored with hojicha, Japanese roasted green tea. It comes in loose leaf or powdered form; the powder ensures thorough distribution of the flavor. I steam the cakes in heatproof teacups, or you can use small ramekins. Individual silicone muffin cups will work too, though the flexible material makes them less sturdy, and the cakes may not rise as high.

## BROWN SUGAR SYRUP

¼ cup plus 2 tablespoons (80 g) packed dark brown sugar

¼ cup (50 g) granulated sugar

½ cup (120 g) water

## PROSPERITY CAKES

1 ½ cups (200 g) all-purpose flour

2 tablespoons (34 g) water-milled glutinous rice flour (see Notes)

2 teaspoons (6 g) active dry yeast

1 teaspoon ground cardamom

1 heaping tablespoon hojicha powder

1 large egg, at room temperature

½ cup (120 g) water

Neutral oil, such as canola or grapeseed

1. **Make the syrup:** Combine the brown sugar, granulated sugar, and water in a small saucepan. Bring to a boil, stirring to dissolve the sugars completely. Set aside to cool.

2. **Make the cakes:** Whisk the all-purpose flour, rice flour, yeast, cardamom, and hojicha powder together in a large bowl. Beat the egg with the water in a separate bowl, then add to the flour mixture and mix. Add the sugar syrup and mix until well combined. (The batter should be thick.) Cover and place in a warm area to rise until doubled in size, approximately 1 ½ hours.

3. Line eight heatproof teacups or small glass or ceramic ramekins with muffin cup liners. Spoon the batter into each prepared cup so it comes three-quarters up the sides.

4. Dip the tip of a chopstick in oil, then draw a cross over the surface of the batter. (This will allow the cakes' signature petals to form.)

5. Set a bamboo steamer over 2 inches of water in a wok or add 2 inches of water to a metal steamer pot and place the steamer basket in the pot. Bring to a boil, then reduce the heat to a brisk simmer. Place the cups in the steamer. Cover and steam on medium-high heat for 20 minutes or until the cakes have risen, the petals have splayed, and the cakes are bouncy to the touch.

6. Serve warm, ideally with a cup of hot tea.

**NOTES:** When making doughs and batters, I prefer measuring by weight because it's more precise than volume, so I highly recommend using a kitchen scale.

The rice flour you are looking for is water-milled glutinous rice flour. The term refers to a specific way of wet-milling rice into flour, allowing for finer processing. My parents used to mill their rice by hand, but now the flour is fairly ubiquitous in Asian grocery marts. ("Water-milled" is usually not specified in English.) I recommend the Erawan brand. Look for the translucent package, labeled with green Thai characters.

炒

*chǎo*

# FRY

清炒蔬菜　Light-Fried Leafy Greens ｜ 71

爆炒白菜　Sichuan Tangy Cabbage Stir-Fry ｜ 72

葱爆牛肉　Beef and Onion Stir-Fry ｜ 75

———

Frying is at the heart of Chinese cuisine, and stir-frying in particular is almost synonymous with Chinese cooking worldwide. Whether it's a quick stir-fry, in which the heat of the pan and a constant tumbling motion prevent the food from absorbing too much fat, or a deep-fry, in which the food is cooked in a pool of very hot oil so it crisps without becoming oily, frying always involves the harnessing of heat with fat. The different types of frying vary according to the level of heat used, the amount of fat, the movement in the pan, the duration of cooking, the amount of sauce, and whether the ingredients are precooked or not. In this chapter, I focus on the more common techniques: stir-fry, deep-fry, pan-fry, and dry-fry.

## 炒  STIR-FRY chǎo

Stir-frying is a beautiful, efficient dance of food in motion. It entails high heat, ingredients that are added in rapid succession while tossing, and, usually, a quick sauce.

The core tenet of stir-frying is to move from step to step without pausing. A few tips:

- Prep all your ingredients and have them at room temperature, so they don't bring the temperature of the wok down and steam rather than fry. Uniform shapes help the food to cook evenly and are aesthetically pleasing.
- Heat the wok before you add the oil (the Chinese say "热锅冷油 *rè guō lěng yóu*" or "hot wok, cold oil"). To test, add a drop of water to the dry wok; it should sizzle and immediately evaporate.
- Wait until you are ready to toss in your ingredients before adding the oil, so it won't get smoky, which can make food bitter. Swirl to coat the wok's surface.

- Stir-frying is not really stirring, but tossing, tumbling, and flipping. This motion allows all the surfaces of the food to touch the wok, necessary for even cooking.
- The amount of food is important—plan for circulation and don't crowd the wok, or the ingredients will steam.
- Consider the cooking time for each of your ingredients. In the case of bok choy and a carrot, the bok choy will cook more quickly and can be tossed in near the end, whereas a carrot will take longer and may even need a quick blanching before being added to the wok.

The basic stir-fry process is:

1. Cook the meat, chicken, seafood, or tofu, remove, and set aside.
2. Bloom (fry) the aromatics in oil to unlock their flavors.
3. Add the vegetables.
4. Return the protein to the wok.
5. Add the sauce.

There are a number of subcategories in stir-fry, with their own variations on that general flow. There are 生炒 *shēng chǎo*, the basic stir-fry with minimal sauce; and 滑炒 *huá chǎo*, a stir-fry that incorporates velveting then stir frying with plenty of sauce. There is 清炒 *qīng chǎo*, a clear stir-fry, usually leafy greens steam-fried in the barest of seasonings such as stock or a splash of Shaoxing wine. In 煸炒 *biān chǎo*, all the ingredients are raw when tossed in the wok. In 熟炒 *shú chǎo*, a "cooked" stir-fry, the meat or seafood is half cooked or mostly cooked before being added, then is stir-fried with the sauce for a final unification. In 干炒 *gān chǎo*, a dry stir-fry (not to be confused with dry-frying, below), the ingredients are marinated, then fried with condiments and seasonings to concentrate the sauce. Velveting, a process called 过油, *guò yóu*, involves first marinating pork, fish, beef, or chicken in a salty, sweet, and aromatic mixture of soy sauce, Shaoxing wine, sugar, and cornstarch for 10 to 20 minutes. This step not only flavors the meat, but also keeps it tender and helps it retain moisture, since the cornstarch coats and insulates it. Then, it's passed through a brief deep-fry – that "passing through oil" – which seals in the moisture and tenderizes the meat. This can then be used in a typical stir-fry.

I would be remiss not to include the famous wok hei, or wok breath, in this discussion. Cantonese chefs add an extra smoky element to their stir-fries with powerful heat, the kind not realistic to achieve in a home kitchen. Chinese professional burners can produce over 100,000 BTUs. Contrast this with the standard American burner, which puts out only around 10,000 BTUs. The intense kiss of the flame is not a prerequisite for a stir-fry, particularly the home-style kind, and in fact in other parts of China, the flavor isn't utilized as much. If you like, you can approximate it by deliberately letting your ingredients sit against the hot pan and blacken.

## 干煸 DRY-FRY *gān biān*

This method capitalizes on the heat of the wok and uses less oil than a regular stir-fry. By scorching or blistering food, it dehydrates and draws out the moisture inside, so subsequent liquid additions, such as a sauce or seasonings), can be absorbed, concentrating the flavor. Dry-fried green beans, 干煸四季豆 *gān biān sì jì dòu*, is perhaps the most famous dish in this method. (**See Dry-Fried Lotus Root and Broccoli, page 96.**)

## 爆 "EXPLODE" OR "BURST" *bào*

When aromatics such as garlic, ginger, or scallion are added to hot oil, they 爆香 *bào xiāng*, "explode into fragrance." The immediate high-temperature sizzle instantly releases all their delicious flavor, transforming the food at that moment of contact. This flash-fry technique, in which the heating time is very short, is also suitable for cooking delicate, fresh foods such as seafood, vegetables, or thinly sliced meat. The technique is also referred to as 油爆 *yóu bào*.

## 煎 PAN-FRY *jiān*

This technique involves frying in a single layer in a pan. The goal is to create a browning reaction by allowing the ingredients to sit in the oil undisturbed, the very opposite of the continuous motion of stir-frying. The term 贴 *tiē*, a sibling of *jiān*, refers to pan-frying on just one side, such as with pan-fried dumplings.

## 炸 DEEP-FRY *zhà*

In this well-known technique, the food is fried in a pool of hot oil, which both cooks it and creates a crispy exterior. I use a thermometer, aiming for 350°F to 375°F. Another way to gauge the temperature is to stick a wooden chopstick in the oil, and if tiny bubbles float rapidly up around it, the heat is adequate. Also within this category is oil-poaching, where you start with a deep-fry, then turn off the heat and allow the residual heat to continue to cook the food. In addition, there is 烹 *pēng*, a double-fry, in which the first deep-fry sets the outside of the food and seals in moisture, then a second fry, usually a stir-fry, adds seasoning or extra crispiness, as in **Sesame-Cumin Fried Chicken (page 99).**

# LIGHT-FRIED LEAFY GREENS

清炒蔬菜 | *qīng chǎo shū cài* | Serves 4

This dish is an excellent way to begin to learn to stir-fry, and it's hard to mess up. You'll often see it called "market greens" on restaurant menus, meaning whatever green is in season. With this method, you're drawing out the innate flavor of the greens and helping express that flavor with a bit of garlic and hot oil. The dish is a great example of why it is important to know your ingredients. A-choy (celtuce leaves) will fry differently from bok choy, which will fry differently from pea shoots. The timing of your stir-fry and visual cues will vary based on which green you choose. The best way to figure this out is by doing it. Do it over and over again until you don't need to watch the clock and can just go by your senses. The greens should be slightly wilted and cooked, but not soft or soggy. Crisp-tender!

1. Heat a wok over medium-high heat until a drop of water evaporates on contact. Add the oil and swirl to coat the wok.

2. Add the garlic and fry until fragrant but not browned, about 30 seconds.

3. Add the greens all at once and quickly stir-fry. Stir-fry until the greens are bright green. Add the salt and a splash of water.

4. Add another liquid if you are so inclined. Cover with a lid and steam for 2 to 3 minutes, until the greens are just tender. (The timing will vary depending on how sturdy or thick they are.)

5. Adjust the seasoning. Serve immediately.

2 tablespoons neutral oil, such as canola or grapeseed

5 garlic cloves, thinly sliced

14 ounces (400 g) leafy greens, such as snow pea shoots, A-choy, bok choy, or tatsoi, washed well and dried, separated into individual leaves (cut large leaves in half or thirds)

½ teaspoon kosher salt, plus more to taste

1 tablespoon Shaoxing wine, 1 tablespoon light soy sauce, or 2 tablespoons flavorful stock (optional)

# SICHUAN TANGY CABBAGE STIR-FRY

爆炒白菜 | *bào chǎo bái cài* | Serves 2 to 4

If I had to pick just one go-to vegetable dish, it would be this. It's a simple, classic Sichuan recipe highlighting the versatility of cabbage that my dad learned from his mom, who is from the province. He told me that the key is to fry the aromatics until they're charred. This step can be smoky, so be sure to have your range hood on. With just a bit of spicy heat, the napa cabbage becomes sweet and slightly wilted, as it soaks up the vinegary flavors from the stir-fry. The dish hits every flavor note: sweet and salty, tangy from black vinegar, and smoky-aromatic from the spices. You can use napa or green cabbage. Napa cabbage is a bit more delicate, and green cabbage has more structure—both have their unique attributes, and I use them interchangeably.

1 pound (455 g) napa or green cabbage (about 1 small head)

1 tablespoon light soy sauce

1 tablespoon black vinegar

1 tablespoon sugar

1 teaspoon cornstarch

½ teaspoon kosher salt

2 tablespoons neutral oil, such as canola or grapeseed

2 dried red Sichuan chile peppers

¼ teaspoon coarsely crushed red Sichuan peppercorns

1 piece star anise

3 garlic cloves, thinly sliced

Ground white pepper

1. Separate the leaves of the cabbage, discarding any bruised outer ones, and rinse thoroughly. Tear or cut the leaves into 1½-inch chunks, keeping the thick stemmier bottom third of the leaves separate from the thinner top two-thirds.

2. Combine the soy sauce, vinegar, sugar, cornstarch, and salt in a small bowl.

3. Heat a wok over high heat until a drop of water evaporates on contact. Add the oil and swirl to coat the wok.

4. Add the chile peppers, Sichuan peppercorns, and star anise and stir-fry until they start to blacken and char.

5. Reduce the heat to medium, then add the garlic and stir-fry quickly until fragrant, about 30 seconds. Add the cabbage stems. Stir-fry for 1 minute or until the stems start to wilt, then add the remaining cabbage and stir-fry for 30 to 60 seconds, until just wilted.

6. Add the sauce and white pepper to taste and stir-fry quickly to combine, another minute or so.

7. Serve hot.

# BEEF AND ONION STIR-FRY

葱爆牛肉 | *cōng bào níu ròu* | Serves 4

**A home-style, humble dish, this beef and onion stir-fry relies on constant, rapid movement and high heat. Make sure your range hood is running, because that high heat is necessary to get a nice sear on the beef and char on the onion. Serve with white rice.**

1. Soak the beef slices in cold water for 5 minutes to remove any blood. Drain and pat dry.

2. **Meanwhile, make the marinade:** Stir together the Shaoxing wine, oyster sauce, soy sauce, and cornstarch in a medium bowl. Place the beef slices in the marinade and set aside for 20 minutes.

3. **Make the sauce:** Stir the water, light and dark soy sauces, sugar, and sesame oil together in a small bowl.

4. Heat a wok over high heat until a drop of water evaporates on contact. With the range hood running, add the neutral oil and swirl to coat.

5. Add the beef to the wok in a single layer and sear undisturbed for about 1 minute, until browned. Discard any remaining marinade.

6. Flip and sear the other side for another minute, then stir-fry for about 30 seconds, until the beef is about three-quarters cooked through. Transfer to a plate.

7. If the wok is dry, add another splash of neutral oil. Add the onion slices and quickly stir-fry until slightly charred but not softened, 60 to 90 seconds.

8. Return the beef to the wok, then add the sauce. Stir-fry until the sauce has cooked down slightly and coats the beef and onion, about 1 minute more. Serve.

### MARINATED STEAK

10 ounces (300 g) flank steak, sliced ¼ inch thick against the grain

2 teaspoons Shaoxing wine

1 teaspoon oyster sauce

1 teaspoon soy sauce

1 teaspoon cornstarch

### SAUCE

¼ cup (60 g) water

1 tablespoon light soy sauce

2 teaspoons dark soy sauce

1 teaspoon sugar

¼ teaspoon toasted sesame oil

2 tablespoons neutral oil, such as canola or grapeseed, plus more as needed

1 sweet (Vidalia) onion, sliced into ¼-inch-thick half-moons (about 1½ to 2 cups/330 g)

**SUBSTITUTE:** I use a sweet onion, but scallions, leeks, or red onion work, too.

# FRIED FARRO WITH LAP CHEONG AND CABBAGE

Serves 4

Fried rice is a gateway dish. Master it and you'll have learned both how to optimize ingredients and the best order to toss them into the wok. In this dish, I take all the genius of fried rice and make it with farro. I love farro's nuttiness and chewiness—when fried with a cured sausage like lap cheong and a sprinkle of smoky paprika, it makes for a hearty, robust dish. (Also see **Fried Rice with Pickled Chiles, Eggs, and Spam, page 241.**)

I start by stir-frying the meat, which renders the fat. Then I add aromatics to the fat to boost its fragrance. Next, I put in the vegetables, starting with the sturdier ones and moving to the more delicate (the sturdier ones require more time in the pan). Finally, I add the cooked grain and toss everything together. This dish is good with or without a fried egg.

1 cup (7 ounces/200 g) un-cooked pearled farro

3 cups (720 g) water

½ teaspoon kosher salt, plus more to taste

1 teaspoon extra-virgin olive oil

3 tablespoons neutral oil, such as canola or grapeseed

4 links lap cheong (4 ounces/115 g total), diced

1 shallot, thinly sliced

3 garlic cloves, roughly chopped

1 teaspoon smoked paprika

½ teaspoon ground turmeric

½ teaspoon freshly ground black pepper, plus more to taste

8 ounces (225 g) napa cabbage, cut into ½-inch slivers

1 teaspoon light soy sauce

½ teaspoon sugar

Grated zest and juice of 1 lemon

4 fried eggs (optional)

1. Rinse the farro and cover with the water in a medium saucepan. Season with the salt and olive oil. Bring to a boil, then reduce the heat to low to maintain a simmer. Cover and cook until the farro is al dente, approximately 25 minutes. Drain and set aside.

2. Heat a wok over medium-high heat until a drop of water evaporates on contact. Add the neutral oil and swirl to coat the wok. Add the lap cheong, stirring often until it begins to brown and the fat has rendered, about
2 minutes.

3. Add the shallot and stir-fry, tossing often, until brown, about 3 minutes. Add the garlic and stir-fry briefly until fragrant. Stir in the paprika, turmeric, and black pepper and allow the spices to bloom in the oil.

4. Fold in the cabbage and cook until just wilted, about 5 minutes, and then let it sit undisturbed for 3 to 5 minutes, until it begins to char. Stir well, then let sit undisturbed for another 90 seconds.

5. Add the farro and stir-fry to combine, then add the soy sauce and sugar and stir-fry. Season with salt and pepper to taste.

6. Remove from the heat, stir in the lemon zest, and season with lemon juice. Serve immediately, topped with a fried egg (if using).

**NOTE:** You can use 2½ cups cooked farro and skip the first step.

**SUBSTITUTE:** If you can't find lap cheong, you can substitute any cured meat for that salty, umami flavor, such as Spanish chorizo.

# GINGERY CHICKEN AND ASPARAGUS STIR-FRY

Serves 4

**This is what a typical weeknight stir-fry looks like in my kitchen. Stir-frying doesn't have to be a sprint to the end (though it often does move quickly)—you can introduce steps such as browning, steaming, or sauce reduction in the same wok, based on the ingredients you are using. I intentionally keep the chicken in larger chunks here so it stays juicy. I let it brown properly before introducing the movement of stir-fry, then finish with a steaming step, partly to let the sauce thicken but also to cook the chicken through.**

1. **Make the ginger water:** Blitz the sliced ginger with the water in a blender. Strain through a fine-mesh sieve. Discard the solids.

2. **Make the chicken:** Cut into 1-inch pieces and toss with the cornstarch, salt, sugar, pepper, and 2 tablespoons of the ginger water. Let sit at room temperature for 10 minutes.

3. **Meanwhile, make the sauce:** Stir together the honey, fish sauce, minced ginger, pepper, and ¼ cup of the ginger water.

4. **Make the stir-fry:** Heat a wok over medium-high heat until a drop of water evaporates on contact. Add the oil and swirl to coat.

5. Add the chicken and spread in a single layer. Let sit undisturbed until the underside is golden brown, about 3 minutes. Use a spatula to turn the chicken and brown the other side, about 3 minutes.

6. Add the asparagus and stir-fry until bright green but still crisp, about 2 minutes.

7. Add the julienned ginger and the sauce and toss to combine.

8. Cover with a lid, turn the heat to low, and simmer for 5 minutes.

9. Remove the lid, stir in the cornstarch slurry, and simmer for another minute or until the sauce thickens enough to coat the back of a spoon.

10. Serve immediately with rice.

## GINGER WATER

Two ¼-inch-thick slices ginger

½ cup (120 g) water

## MARINATED CHICKEN

1 pound (455 g) boneless, skinless chicken thighs

1 tablespoon cornstarch

1 teaspoon kosher salt

½ teaspoon sugar

½ teaspoon ground black pepper

## GINGER-HONEY SAUCE

2 tablespoons honey

1 teaspoon fish sauce

1 teaspoon minced peeled ginger

½ teaspoon ground black pepper

## STIR-FRY

2 tablespoons neutral oil

10 ounces (300 g) asparagus, sliced on an angle into 1-inch pieces

Two ¼-inch-thick slices peeled ginger, julienned

1 tablespoon cornstarch mixed with 2 tablespoons ginger water

Steamed rice

# GARLICKY RADICCHIO AND PORK STIR-FRY

Serves 4

This dish is more about the radicchio than the pork, which is just there to contribute savory umami. The bit of spicy honey butter added at the end counters the lovely bitterness of the leaf, highlighting rather than diminishing it. With this dish, you'll see how heat can transform this vegetable and how you can use complementary additions (pork for savory umami, honey for sweetness) to balance a dish.

## MARINATED PORK

1 teaspoon cornstarch

1 teaspoon Shaoxing wine

1 teaspoon light soy sauce

½ teaspoon sugar

4 ounces (115 g) pork loin, cut into ¼-inch-wide, 2-inch-long strips

## SPICY HONEY BUTTER

2 tablespoons unsalted butter

1 teaspoon red pepper flakes or gochugaru

¼ teaspoon smoked paprika

2 teaspoons honey


1 small head radicchio (about 8 ounces/225 g)

2 tablespoons neutral oil, such as canola or grapeseed, plus more as needed

4 garlic cloves, thinly sliced

¼ teaspoon crushed red Sichuan peppercorns

2 scallions, trimmed and cut into 1-inch segments

½ teaspoon kosher salt

Juice of 1 lemon

1. **Marinate the pork:** Combine the cornstarch, Shaoxing wine, soy sauce, and sugar in a medium bowl, then add the pork and toss. Set aside for 15 minutes.

2. **Make the butter:** Melt the butter in a small saucepan over medium heat, then stir in the red pepper flakes or gochugaru and the smoked paprika. Remove from the heat, stir in the honey, and set aside.

3. Remove and discard any damaged outer leaves from the radicchio. Cut the radicchio into quarters, then remove the tough cores from the quarters. Tear the leaves into pieces—I like them a bit larger than bite-sized.

4. Heat a wok over medium-high heat until a drop of water evaporates on contact. Add the oil and swirl to coat the wok.

5. Add the pork and stir-fry until it is just cooked through but not browned, 2 to 3 minutes. Transfer to a plate and set aside.

6. If the wok is dry, add another splash of oil. Add the garlic and stir-fry until fragrant, about 30 seconds. Add the crushed Sichuan peppercorns and scallions and stir-fry briefly.

7. Turn the heat to high and add the radicchio to the wok. Season with the salt and stir-fry until the radicchio just begins to wilt.

8. Return the pork to the wok and toss to combine.

9. Remove from the heat, season with lemon juice to taste, then drizzle with the spicy honey butter. Serve.

# BLACK PEPPER BEEF AND SHISHITO RICE CAKES

Serves 4

I used to order fried rice cakes in Chinese restaurants instead of cooking them at home—until I discovered how easy they are to stir-fry. They become warm and soft so they soak up the flavors of a sauce and other ingredients. Be careful though: overcook them and they turn mushy. You're aiming for a texture that is soft but chewy, not shatteringly crisp. To get the timing right, first stir-fry the ingredients that contribute flavor: brown the beef, blister the peppers (thereby adding some mellow heat), and fry the aromatics. Add the rice cakes and sauce only when you're ready for everything to come together.

1. If using fresh rice cakes, soak them in water for 10 minutes so they loosen and separate, then drain, to give them time to lose moisture.

2. **Marinate the beef:** Cut the flank steak along the grain into 1-inch-wide strips. Then slice against the grain into ¼-inch-thick pieces. Stir together the cornstarch, soy sauce, and Shaoxing wine in a bowl. Add the steak slices, toss to coat, and set aside to marinate for 15 to 20 minutes.

3. **Meanwhile, make the sauce:** Stir together the water, soy sauce, sugar, and pepper in a small bowl and set aside.

4. Heat a wok over high heat until a drop of water evaporates on contact. Add the oil and swirl to coat the wok.

5. Add the beef in a single layer and let sear very briefly (less than 30 seconds), then stir-fry until just browned. Do it in batches if necessary. Transfer to a plate.

6. Add a splash of oil to the wok if it looks dry, then add the shishitos, also working in batches if necessary, until they are blistered all over. Remove from the wok and set aside.

7. Add the garlic, ginger, and the white parts of the scallion to the wok and stir-fry for 1 minute or until fragrant.

8. Return the shishito peppers and beef to the wok, along with the rice cakes. Add the black pepper sauce and stir to combine. Reduce the heat to medium, cover, and cook for 4 to 5 minutes, until most of the sauce has been absorbed. Remove the lid and stir-fry for 2 to 3 minutes, until the rice cakes are tender and chewy. Sprinkle with the scallion green slivers and serve.

**SUBSTITUTES:** You can substitute sirloin steak or rib eye for the flank steak.

Instead of the vacuum-sealed fresh rice cakes, you can use dried or frozen rice cakes. They will take a bit longer to cook; follow the directions on the package.

1 pound (455 g) vacuum-packed fresh rice cakes

## MARINATED BEEF

12 ounces (340 g) flank steak

1 tablespoon cornstarch

1 tablespoon light soy sauce

1 tablespoon Shaoxing wine

## BLACK PEPPER SAUCE

¼ cup (60 g) water

3 tablespoons light soy sauce

2 tablespoons sugar

1½ teaspoons freshly ground black pepper

2 tablespoons neutral oil, such as canola or grapeseed, plus more as needed

6 ounces (170 g) shishito peppers, stemmed and halved lengthwise.

2 garlic cloves, minced

1 teaspoon minced peeled ginger

2 scallions, trimmed, white parts finely chopped and green parts cut into 2-inch slivers

# SAUSAGE AND CAULIFLOWER CHOW MEIN

Serves 4

**Stir-fried noodles are endlessly riffable. Chinese cauliflower is delicate and sweet, making it a good complement to Italian sausage. This vegetable also has thinner stems than regular cauliflower, so it's perfect for stir-frying. The sausage adds so much flavor that you won't need to season the dish much.**

1 medium Chinese cauliflower (1 pound/455 g), torn into bite-sized pieces

1 pound (455 g) fresh wheat or egg lo mein noodles

2 tablespoons neutral oil, such as canola or grapeseed, plus more as needed

8 ounces (225 g) hot Italian sausage, loose or removed from the casings

3 garlic cloves, minced

2 tablespoons light soy sauce

2 teaspoons sugar

2 tablespoons unsalted butter

2 scallions, trimmed and thinly sliced

Lemon wedge

Kosher salt and freshly ground black pepper

1. Bring a large pot of water to a boil over high heat and prepare an ice bath. Blanch the cauliflower until cooked but still crisp-tender, about 4 minutes. Transfer to the ice bath with a slotted spoon.

2. Bring the water back to a boil, then add the noodles. Cook until al dente. Measure out 2 tablespoons of the cooking water and set aside. Drain the noodles and set them aside.

3. Drain the cauliflower and pat dry.

4. Heat a wok over medium-high heat until a drop of water evaporates on contact. Add the oil and swirl to coat. Add the sausage and use a spatula to flatten it out into a thin layer. Cook undisturbed for 3 to 5 minutes, until browned, then use the spatula to break it up into bite-sized pieces. Stir-fry until all sides are browned and crispy, about 3 minutes more, then transfer to a paper towel–lined plate.

5. If the wok is dry, add another splash of oil. Add the garlic and stir-fry until fragrant, about 30 seconds. Add the cauliflower and stir-fry until it begins to brown, 3 to 4 minutes. Add the noodles and sausage and toss to combine thoroughly. Add the soy sauce, sugar, and butter and continue to toss as the butter melts. Let sit for 5 minutes so the noodles are slightly charred. Remove the wok from the heat.

6. Add the scallions and top with a squeeze of lemon juice. Season with salt and pepper, if necessary. Serve immediately.

**SUBSTITUTES:** You can substitute crumbled firm tofu or another ground meat, such as pork or lamb, for the sausage.

If you can't find Chinese cauliflower, feel free to use ordinary cauliflower, but make sure to tear it into thin pieces.

# STIR-FRIED POTATO SLIVERS WITH LEMONGRASS AND JALAPEÑO

Serves 2

**Potatoes are often mashed or boiled, but they are delightful stir-fried. They're traditionally sliced into thin slivers or shreds, then stir-fried with aromatics such as scallions, or in the Sichuan region, chile peppers, and often scrambled eggs. Rinsing the slivers in water first makes for a crisp-tender texture, leaving just enough starch behind so that they can crisp up nicely. The fragrant, floral lemongrass flavor is balanced by the zing of jalapeños.**

1. Soak the potato slivers in cold water for 10 minutes to remove excess starch and keep them crisp during stir-frying. Place the slivers in a colander, rinse with cold water until the water runs clear, and let them drain.

2. Meanwhile, beat the eggs with the soy sauce in a small bowl.

3. Heat a wok or large nonstick skillet over high heat until a drop of water evaporates on contact. Add 1 tablespoon of the oil. When it shimmers, add the eggs. Scramble them occasionally, until big, fluffy, just-cooked curds form. Transfer the eggs to a clean bowl and set aside.

4. Use a paper towel to wipe out the pan, then add the remaining tablespoon oil. When it shimmers, add the lemongrass and jalapeño and stir-fry for 30 seconds. Add the garlic and stir-fry for another 30 seconds. Add the potato slivers and stir-fry until they start to become soft and translucent but still retain some crunch, 1½ to 2 minutes. Add the fish sauce, sugar, and white pepper and stir-fry until thoroughly incorporated, about 1½ minutes more. The potato should be firm but just cooked through, like an al dente noodle.

5. Add the scrambled eggs and scallion, toss to combine, then immediately transfer to a plate and serve.

1 large russet potato (about 11½ ounces/325 g), peeled and julienned into ⅛-inch-thick slivers

2 large eggs

1 teaspoon light soy sauce

2 tablespoons neutral oil, such as canola or grapeseed, divided

2 tablespoons minced lemongrass (from the white bottom 2 inches of 1 peeled stalk)

1 jalapeño, seeded and thinly sliced crosswise

1 garlic clove, minced

1 tablespoon fish sauce

1 tablespoon sugar

½ teaspoon ground white pepper

1 scallion, trimmed and thinly sliced

**NOTE:** To julienne, I use a knife, though you can use a mandoline. And it's OK to give yourself grace and have some uneven pieces.

# PAN-FRIED CRISPY MUSHROOM–SOY SAUCE NOODLES

Serves 2 generously

**Chow mein, the Cantonese romanization of 炒面 *chǎo miàn* in Mandarin, aka stir-fried noodles, comes in many different flavors and is well-known in Chinese American cuisine. In this variation on a Cantonese classic that is popular in Hong Kong cafés, the noodles are pan-fried to give them an intermittently crispy but tender texture. I give the dish a slight twist that leans its profile away from salty soy sauce toward umami, earthy mushrooms by using a mix of fungi for a multifaceted mushroom flavor. The noodles are seasoned with just the right amount of soy sauce, which caramelizes in the wok.**

8 ounces (225 g) dried Hong Kong–style egg noodles

4 to 5 tablespoons neutral oil, divided

7 ounces (200 g) mixed mushrooms, such as shiitake, oyster, and/or beech, cleaned and trimmed, sliced or torn into 2-inch pieces if necessary (about 3 cups)

1 tablespoon light soy sauce

1 tablespoon dark soy sauce

1 tablespoon Shaoxing rice wine

1 teaspoon sugar

¼ teaspoon ground white pepper

2 tablespoons unsalted butter, divided

2 scallions, trimmed, whites and greens separated and very thinly sliced

2 garlic cloves, minced

1 cup (100 g) mung bean sprouts

Truffle oil or truffle zest to finish (optional)

1. Soak the egg noodles in hot water for 2 to 3 minutes, until they untangle and are soft. Rinse with cold water and set aside to drain.

2. Heat 3 tablespoons of the neutral oil in a wok over medium-high heat. When it shimmers, add the mushrooms in a single layer—in 2 batches if necessary so you don't crowd them—and fry, stirring occasionally, until browned all over, 8 to 12 minutes. Transfer them to a paper towel–lined plate to drain.

3. While the mushrooms cook, combine both soy sauces, the Shaoxing wine, the sugar, and the white pepper in a small bowl and set aside.

4. If the pan seems dry, add another tablespoon of the neutral oil. Add the egg noodles, spreading them out in an even layer across the bottom of the pan, pressing them down gently against the pan so they get maximum contact with the hot surface.

5. Add 1 tablespoon of the butter and use cooking chopsticks to move it around the perimeter of the pan, until fully melted.

6. Let the noodles cook undisturbed. After about 5 minutes, once the edges of the noodles begin to turn golden and you can smell them starting to toast and char, carefully turn the noodles over in sections. Add the remaining butter and brown the noodles on the other side. They should be crispy and partially charred in parts but still relatively soft. Transfer them to a bowl and set aside.

7. Turn the heat to high. Add the remaining tablespoon neutral oil to the pan, then add the white parts of the scallion and the garlic and let them sizzle until fragrant, about 30 seconds.

8. Reduce the heat to low, return the egg noodles to the pan, then add the soy sauce mixture, stirring to coat.

9. After the noodles are mixed with the sauce and are golden brown, increase the heat to high and let the noodles crisp up and char some more, stirring once or twice, about 2 minutes.

10. Add the scallion greens and the bean sprouts and stir-fry until the bean sprouts are just wilted and translucent, 1 to 2 minutes more.

11. Return the mushrooms to the pan and toss to combine, then remove from the heat.

12. Finish with truffle oil or zest (if using), and serve.

# SRIRACHA SHRIMP TOAST

Serves 4; makes 16 pieces

**These spicy, cheesy, decadent toasts are spread with a mixture of chopped shrimp, butter, a generous amount of sriracha, and sharp cheddar, and pan-fried. I like milk bread as the base, but you can substitute any bread with a soft crumb. Hand-chopping the shrimp is best so they retain some texture. I often serve the toasts as snacks or as a carb-y accompaniment to meals; they also make delicious appetizers.**

1. Mince the shrimp with a cleaver, smashing them occasionally with the flat side so you have a coarse paste. Transfer to a bowl.

2. Mix in the garlic, butter, egg white, sriracha, Shaoxing wine, soy sauce, sesame oil, cornstarch, sugar, and salt. Fold in the scallions, ginger, and cheddar cheese. You should have a sticky paste.

3. Spread the paste in a thick, even layer across each slice of bread.

4. Cut each slice of bread into four 2-inch squares, for a total of 16 pieces.

5. Put the sesame seeds in a shallow dish and gently dip the shrimp side of the toasts into the sesame seeds to coat.

6. Heat the neutral oil in a large nonstick skillet over medium heat until shimmering. Place the toasts in the skillet, sesame side down, turn the heat to medium-low, and fry until the shrimp layer is golden and cooked through, 7 to 10 minutes.

7. Turn the toasts bread side down and cook until golden brown, 2 to 3 minutes.

8. Transfer to a serving plate and serve immediately.

8 ounces (225 g) shrimp, peeled and deveined

2 garlic cloves, minced

1 tablespoon unsalted butter, at room temperature

1 large egg white

1 tablespoon sriracha

2 teaspoons Shaoxing wine

1 teaspoon light soy sauce

½ teaspoon toasted sesame oil

2 teaspoons cornstarch

1 teaspoon sugar

½ teaspoon kosher salt

2 scallions, trimmed and finely chopped

1 teaspoon minced peeled ginger

4 ounces (115 g) sharp cheddar, grated (1 packed cup)

Four 1-inch-thick slices Milk Bread (homemade, **page 256,** or store-bought)

2 tablespoons toasted sesame seeds

2 tablespoons neutral oil, such as canola or grapeseed

**NOTE:** Shrimp are easier to chop when partially frozen. You can buy deveined, peeled frozen shrimp and partially thaw them, then chop, or peel and devein your raw shrimp and freeze just to firm up the flesh a little for chopping. Or you can use a food processor instead of hand chopping. Pulse in short bursts to keep some of the texture.

**SUBSTITUTE:** Challah, brioche, and even thin sandwich bread are suitable substitutes for milk bread; any bread with a soft, slightly sweet crumb will work well. Avoid sturdier breads with large holes in the crumb or robust crusts.

# CORN MOCHI FRITTERS

Makes 12 fritters

At the height of summer, when big piles of corn appear in the produce aisle, I look for the ones with dark brown, not-too-dry silk at the end of the husk, indicating the kernels inside will be particularly sweet. These fritters taste like the essence of the corn flavor. They're made from a concentrated corn liquid thickened with fine rice flour and dotted with the kernels. Pan-frying quickly crisps the fritters, resulting in a delightfully chewy, crispy exterior and a springy interior, courtesy of the rice flour.

8 ounces (225 g) fresh corn kernels from 1 to 2 ears, or thawed frozen kernels (1½ cups), divided

½ cup (120 g) water

2 tablespoons unsalted butter, melted and cooled

1 tablespoon light soy sauce

1½ cups (180 g) water-milled glutinous rice flour (I prefer the Erawan brand; look for the green label), plus more as needed

3 tablespoons sugar

2 scallions, trimmed and chopped

Neutral oil, such as canola or grapeseed

Flaky salt

## DIPPING SAUCE

1 tablespoon maple syrup

1 tablespoon dark soy sauce

1. Combine ½ cup (75 g) of the corn and the water in a blender and blitz on high speed until smooth. Strain through a fine-mesh sieve and discard the solids. You should have at least ½ cup corn juice.

2. Stir together 6 tablespoons of the corn juice, the melted butter, light soy sauce, rice flour, sugar, scallions, and the remaining whole corn kernels to form a dough. Add more flour as needed until the dough has the consistency of Play-Doh. It should hold its shape and not stick to your hands. Wrap the dough in plastic and rest it at room temperature for 30 minutes.

3. Divide the dough into quarters. Working with one quarter at a time and keeping the rest wrapped in plastic, cut it into three equal pieces. Roll each piece between your palms to make a ball. Repeat with the remaining dough until you have 12 balls, keeping all the dough balls covered loosely with plastic once they're formed.

4. Heat 2 tablespoons oil in a large nonstick skillet over medium-high heat until shimmering.

5. Working in batches, smush each ball into a ¼-inch-thick round between your palms, and place in the hot oil. Cook only as many fritters as will fit in a single layer in your pan. Fry until golden brown all over, 3 to 4 minutes per side. Transfer the fritters to a paper towel–lined plate. Immediately sprinkle with flaky salt. Repeat as necessary with the remaining dough and more oil.

6. **Make the dipping sauce:** Mix the maple syrup and dark soy sauce together in a small bowl.

7. Serve the fritters drizzled with the sauce, or serve the sauce on the side for dipping.

# DAD'S BALSAMIC FRIED EGGS

Makes 2 eggs

**This dish is so straightforward that it feels almost like cheating. My father always topped my breakfast noodle soup with these special eggs before I took an exam. Exceedingly easy, they are full of caramelized flavor. The soup was simple: usually chicken stock mixed with a dash of soy sauce, black vinegar, a shake of ground white pepper, and a tiny bit of chile crisp.**

1. Stir together the balsamic vinegar and honey in a small bowl. Set aside.

2. Heat the wok over medium-high heat, then add the oil and swirl to coat.

3. When the oil shimmers, crack the eggs into the wok and let sit undisturbed until the edges start to turn opaque—this will happen almost immediately.

4. Turn the heat to low and drizzle the balsamic vinegar mixture around the circumference of the eggs, not over them (the shape of the wok will help the sauce pool around the eggs).

5. Remove from the heat, cover with a lid, and let sit for another 2 minutes or until the egg whites are just set but the yolks are still runny.

6. Sprinkle with sesame seeds, flaky salt and pepper and serve immediately.

2 teaspoons balsamic vinegar

½ teaspoon honey

1 tablespoon neutral oil, such as canola or grapeseed

2 large eggs

Sesame seeds

Flaky salt and freshly ground black pepper

# DRY-FRIED LOTUS ROOT AND BROCCOLI

Serves 4

**Sturdy yet crisp, lotus root holds up well in all manner of dishes—boiled in soup, stir-fried and coated in sauce, or dry-fried. Dry-frying doesn't necessarily mean the dish is dry—it means letting the ingredient blister and shrivel a bit, evaporating its moisture, so it is primed for absorbing any sauce. In the case of lotus root, dry-frying not only crisps it but deepens its flavor. As for the broccoli, stir-frying can produce a variety of flavors and textures, depending on the level of heat, the length of cooking time, and the way the broccoli is cut. I like to let the thinner strips sit in the pan, without stirring them, so they sear and brown.**

2 tablespoons white rice vinegar

One 4-inch piece lotus root (8 ounces/225 g), peeled and cut into ¼-inch matchsticks

1 tablespoon light soy sauce

1 tablespoon maple syrup

1 small head broccoli (8 ounces/225 g), stem peeled and cut into 2- to 2½-inch-long, ¼-inch-thick matchsticks, crown cut into thin florets

1 tablespoon neutral oil, such as canola or grapeseed, plus more as needed

4 garlic cloves, minced

1 teaspoon minced peeled ginger

4 dried red Sichuan chile peppers, stemmed and roughly chopped

Kosher salt and ground white pepper

1. Add the white rice vinegar to a bowl of cold water. Add the lotus root strips and soak for 15 minutes.

2. Combine the soy sauce and maple syrup in a small bowl and set aside.

3. Bring a saucepan of water to a boil. Drain the lotus root, then blanch for 1 minute. Drain. Pat dry thoroughly and set aside.

4. Heat a wok or large skillet over medium-high heat until a drop of water evaporates on contact. When the pan is hot, add 1 tablespoon oil and swirl to coat.

5. Add the lotus root strips and let sit in the pan undisturbed until the edges begin to brown and the vegetable begins to char and shrivel slightly, 4 to 6 minutes. Transfer to a bowl.

6. Repeat with the broccoli until it blisters, 4 to 6 minutes. Transfer to the bowl with the lotus root.

7. Add another splash of the oil to the pan and quickly stir-fry the garlic and ginger. Add the chile peppers and stir-fry until aromatic, about 30 seconds.

8. Add the soy-maple sauce and let it bubble briefly (less than 30 seconds), then return the lotus root and broccoli to the pan. Toss until they are coated in sauce, then let sit undisturbed for an additional minute to encourage a final char. Remove from the heat and season with salt and white pepper to taste. Serve.

**NOTE:** Look for lotus root that is firm without any obvious soft spots or bruising.

# SESAME-CUMIN FRIED CHICKEN

Serves 4

**Deep-frying often involves a double-fry technique. That method has been traditionally used in Shanghai for shrimp and fish steaks, and it works especially well for chicken. An initial fry at a low temperature seals in the juices and sets the exterior, creating a light coating. Then a second fry at a higher temperature cooks the chicken through and amps up the crispiness. The coating here is seasoned with cumin and gets texture from crushed sesame seeds.**

1. **Marinate the chicken:** Cut the chicken into 1½- to 2-inch chunks. Combine the scallions, garlic, ginger, salt, white pepper, Shaoxing wine, sesame oil, and soy sauce in a medium bowl. Add the chicken and toss to coat. Cover and marinate in the fridge for at least 4 hours or overnight.

2. An hour before cooking, remove the chicken from the fridge and bring to room temperature.

3. **Meanwhile, make the breading:** Crush the sesame seeds with the sugar with a mortar and pestle, or pulse in a food processor, until a coarse powder forms. Mix the sesame seed mixture with the potato starch and cumin in a shallow bowl. Set aside.

4. **Make the cumin salt:** Stir together and set aside.

5. **Make the lemon mayo, if using:** Combine the mayo, lemon juice, and garlic in a small bowl. Refrigerate until you're ready to serve.

6. Heat 2 inches neutral oil to 335°F in a large, deep, heavy pot. Set a wire cooling rack inside a baking sheet, and line a large plate with a few layers of paper towels. Prepare another one for after frying.

7. Working in batches, remove chicken from marinade, letting any liquid drip off each piece, and place chicken in breading mix. Flip to coat thoroughly in the breading, then set on first prepared wire rack.

8. When oil reaches 335°F, gently coat the chicken with more breading mixture, then carefully slip it into the hot oil. Fry for 90 seconds or until the chicken is pale golden and slightly puffy, then transfer to the second wire rack using a slotted spoon.

9. Repeat the breading and frying process with the remaining chicken, allowing the oil to reach 335°F between batches and using a slotted spoon to remove any loose breading from the hot oil.

10. Once the initial frying is complete, increase the oil temperature to 350°F.

11. Fry each batch again for 3 to 5 minutes, gently turning occasionally, until the chicken is evenly golden brown and has an internal temperature of at least 165°F. Place the fried chicken on the paper towel–lined plate to drain, then sprinkle with the cumin salt.

12. Serve with the lemon mayonnaise, if desired.

2 scallions, roughly chopped

3 large garlic cloves, peeled and smashed

2 teaspoons grated ginger

1 teaspoon kosher salt

¼ teaspoon ground white pepper

2 tablespoons Shaoxing wine

1 tablespoon toasted sesame oil

1 tablespoon light soy sauce

1½ to 2 pounds (680 to 910 g) boneless, skinless chicken thighs

¼ cup (37 g) white sesame seeds

2 tablespoons sugar

¾ cup (120 g) potato starch

1 teaspoon ground cumin

## CUMIN SALT

½ teaspoon kosher salt

½ teaspoon freshly ground black pepper

½ teaspoon ground cumin

¼ teaspoon smoked paprika

## LEMON MAYONNAISE

¼ cup (65 g) Kewpie mayonnaise

Juice of 1 lemon

1 garlic clove, minced

Neutral oil

煮

*zhǔ*

# BOIL

蒜泥白切肉 White-Cut Pork Belly | 105
腐乳A菜 Seasoned A-Choy with Furu Sauce | 106

———

Water is fundamental in cooking: a readily available tool, and not just for washing food. A slew of cooking techniques—simmering, flash-poaching, boiling, blanching, and poaching—capitalize on water's potential, with differences in the level of the heat and the duration of the ingredients' immersion in it.

## SIMMER 煨 *wēi* / 煮 *zhǔ*

This method cooks food by submerging it in gently bubbling but not fully boiling water. The heat is carefully adjusted to maintain a brisk little gurgling. Congee, for example, is cooked this way—the rice is not cooked at a rolling boil but is simmered until the starch is broken down. Another example is simmered greens, which are cooked until they're soft and have mellowed in flavor. Contrast this with blanching, where the greens are briefly boiled so they retain some crispy crunch. Simmering also differs from braising, which uses the lowest heat, a (mostly) enclosed space for heat retention, and importantly, a specially made braising liquid.

## FLASH-POACH 水爆 *shuǐ bào*

Similar to "exploding in oil," this technique uses the shock of heat. Usually the ingredients have been sliced thinly enough so they cook instantly once they've been submerged. This is the concept behind hot pot, where you take thinly sliced meat, dip it into boiling water, and lift it out immediately.

## BOIL 白煮 *bái zhǔ*

This method refers to cooking food in boiling water. It takes more time than flash-poaching, and the ingredients are generally thicker. Cooking this way preserves a food's natural taste. Ingredients can be cooked in aromatic water until tender, with a dipping sauce or a dressing added after the fact. With stronger-flavored meats, aromatics and often wine are used in the liquid, leaving them clean-tasting, tender, and ready to be seasoned. One small move that adds shine and flavor to a dish is to add a tiny dollop of fat (such as toasted sesame oil) so that when the food is lifted out of the water, it gets coated with the fat and fragrance. This is the reason a fat like lard is added to soup noodles. While 白煮 *bái zhǔ* means "to boil," the food isn't actually cooked at a high rolling boil the whole time; rather, a gentle bubbling is maintained. 白 *bái* means white. This refers to the fact that food is cooked in water, as opposed to a broth or a liquid seasoned with soy sauce. This gives the food being cooked the spotlight.

## BLANCH 白灼 *bái zhuó*

Blanching can be used to precook a vegetable (断生 *duàn shēng*, to "break rawness") or meat (燙 *tàng*, "scald"), until 80 percent done, usually before stir-frying. As a stand-alone cooking method, blanching is a quick, simple way to cook greens while preserving their color and taste. Water is brought to a boil, the greens are dipped in for a brief amount of time, shocked in an ice bath, then seasoned. I often blanch greens when I'm throwing together a dish, particularly when I'm using the wok for something else.

## POACH 水煮 *shuǐ zhǔ* / 白切 *bái qiē*

Poaching requires high initial heat to kick off the cooking process, then the heat is turned off and the food is allowed to steep. This doesn't stop the cooking, since the residual heat retained in the water continues to very gently cook the food. The method is famously used with chicken, resulting in a silky, tender flesh with minimal effort. White cut (白切 *bái qiē*) describes a specific type of poaching: very clean, with minimal seasoning. Many Chinese names originate from visual descriptions—in this one, the color white

# WHITE-CUT PORK BELLY

蒜泥白切肉 | *suàn ní bái qiē ròu* | Serves 4

This traditional dish is a lovely example of poaching. It's easy, straightforward, and beautiful in its purity. The word "white" signifies that the food is prepared in such a way as to highlight its intrinsic flavors, without soy sauce, which would darken the meat (as in red-cooked pork). The pork belly is poached briefly, then allowed to cool slowly in the liquid, which continues to cook it. It does not melt off the bones (for that, **see Dōng Pō Ròu, page 133**), but is soft and a bit chewy, and holds its shape. The dipping sauce is classic and can be used for any kind of meat cooked this way.

1. Fill a large saucepan with water. Add the scallions, ginger, star anise, and Shaoxing wine and bring to a boil. Reduce the heat and simmer for 5 minutes to infuse the water with the flavors.

2. Add the pork belly. Bring back to a boil, then reduce the heat to the lowest setting to maintain a gently bubbling simmer. Cover and cook for 15 minutes or until cooked through.

3. Remove the pork belly from the water and transfer to a plate. Let sit until just cool enough to handle, 15 to 20 minutes. (Discard the simmering water and flavorings.)

4. **Meanwhile, make the dipping sauce:** Combine the chile peppers, garlic, soy sauce, water, and sugar in a small saucepan over medium heat. Bring to a simmer, let bubble for 1 minute, then remove from the heat. Stir in the sesame oil.

5. Use a sharp knife to slice the warm pork belly into very thin slices (about 1/8 inch thick). Arrange on a plate and serve with the dipping sauce.

2 scallions, trimmed and cut into 2- to 3-inch pieces

Two 1/4-inch-thick slices ginger

1 piece star anise

2 tablespoons Shaoxing wine

14 ounces (400 g) boneless pork belly (skin on) in one 1 1/2-inch-wide strip

## DIPPING SAUCE

2 red Thai chile peppers, stemmed and roughly chopped

3 garlic cloves, minced

2 tablespoons light soy sauce

1 tablespoon water

2 teaspoons sugar

1/4 teaspoon toasted sesame oil

**NOTE:** In Asian grocery stores, pork belly is often sold in a strip that is the ideal width for this recipe.

# SEASONED A-CHOY WITH FURU SAUCE

腐乳A菜 | *fŭ rŭ A cài* | Serves 4

**I hope you'll reach for this recipe often when you're considering how to cook greens. A-choy (celtuce) leaves have a mild peppery taste. Blanched, they retain their freshness; they're then seasoned with a garlicky sauce.**

**A-choy leaves can be quite long. You can leave them whole and serve them with scissors, as they do in dim sum restaurants. Or you can just chop them in half before blanching, as I usually do.**

10½ ounces (300 g) A-choy
leaves (about 2½ bunches)

1 tablespoon kosher salt

Toasted sesame oil

2 tablespoons light soy sauce

1½ teaspoons white fermented
bean curd (*dòu fŭ rŭ;*
about 1½ cubes/9 g)

1 tablespoon sugar

½ teaspoon ground white pepper

1 tablespoon neutral oil,
such as canola or grapeseed

3 garlic cloves, minced

1. Wash the A-choy leaves and drain thoroughly. If the leaves are long, you can chop them in half if you want.

2. Bring a large pot of water to a boil and prepare an ice water bath. When the water boils, add the salt and a drizzle of sesame oil. Add the greens to the boiling water and use cooking chopsticks or tongs to push them down into the water. Once they're bright green, 60 to 90 seconds, immediately transfer them to the ice water until they're cool enough to handle. Drain well, gently squeeze out any extra water, then transfer to a serving dish.

3. Mix together the soy sauce, fermented bean curd, sugar, and white pepper in a small bowl.

4. Heat a wok over medium-high heat until a drop of water evaporates on contact. Add the neutral oil and swirl to coat. Add the garlic and stir-fry until fragrant, about 30 seconds. Turn the heat to the lowest setting. Pour in the sauce, stir, and let bubble for 1 minute.

5. Pour the sauce over the greens and serve.

**NOTE:** I love the funky taste of white furu (fermented tofu, *dòu fŭ rŭ;* see **page 16**), which adds complexity to the sauce. If you can't find it, feel free to omit it and use just the garlic.

# SIMMERED BOK CHOY

Serves 2 generously or 4 with smaller portions

**Deceptively simple and vibrantly flavorful, this dish draws from my roots as a second-generation Shanghainese. I first tasted it in Hang Zhou, near Shanghai. The chef had used the youngest tendrils of bok choy, with leaves the size of a finger. While I can't find bok choy that small here in the US, this recipe works well with ordinary Shanghai bok choy. It's simmered in a flavorful stock, which it absorbs, and as it cooks down it loses its fibrous crunch and becomes silky. This is now one of my favorite ways to enjoy bok choy.**

1. Gently smash the ginger with the flat side of your cleaver to release its flavors.

2. Pull all the outer leaves off the bok choy until just the central baby bulb remains. Discard any shriveled leaves. Trim off the base of the bulb and quarter it. Slice or tear the remaining leaves lengthwise into strips about ½ inch wide. Rinse the bok choy well in a colander under running water to remove any grit.

3. Bring the stock to a boil in a large saucepan over high heat. Turn the heat down to a simmer. Add the ginger and miso and stir. Taste and adjust the seasonings. Add the salt, if using.

4. Add the bok choy leaves and simmer until the whites of the stalks are soft and tender, 7 to 10 minutes, stirring occasionally with cooking chopsticks or tongs. Do not let the stock boil.

5. With a ladle, transfer the bok choy and stock to a serving bowl. Sprinkle with white pepper to taste, and drizzle with the sesame oil.

Two ⅛-inch-thick slices ginger

1 pound (455 g) Shanghai bok choy (4 or 5 medium bulbs)

2 cups (480 g) unsalted chicken stock, or any stock you have

1 tablespoon white (shiro) miso

1 teaspoon kosher salt, plus more to taste (omit if using salted stock)

Ground white pepper

2 or 3 drops toasted sesame oil

**NOTE:** You'll often find a variety of bok choys available in Asian markets, usually differentiated by size. Shanghai bok choy is jade colored and medium in size, whereas baby bok choy has more milky-white stalks and is smaller in size. You can use them fairly interchangeably.

# STICKY RICE RISOTTO WITH KABOCHA AND CRISPY ROASTED BRUSSELS SPROUTS

Serves 4

**Short-grain glutinous rice is known for its characteristic sticky texture, in which each grain of rice clings to the other. This cooking method liberates its plentiful starch and creates a creamy consistency reminiscent of risotto. I've adapted my favorite congee technique here, by flavoring the rice with kabocha squash, which melts into the porridge. Kabocha is a wonderful squash for this. Dense but sweet and slightly nutty, it cooks down into a puree and incorporates itself easily.**

1½ cups (345 g) glutinous rice, such as sweet rice or sticky rice

½ small kabocha squash (1½ pounds / 675 g)

2 tablespoons extra-virgin olive oil

½ large white onion, finely chopped (1 cup / 170 g)

3 garlic cloves, minced

½ cup (120 g) water

½ cup (120 g) dry white wine

3 cups (720 g) unsalted chicken stock

4 tablespoons (½ stick; 115 g) unsalted butter, cut into pieces

½ cup (50 g) freshly grated Parmesan cheese

Kosher salt and freshly ground black pepper

## BRUSSELS SPROUTS

8 ounces (225 g) Brussels sprouts, trimmed and thinly sliced (3 cups)

2 tablespoons extra-virgin olive oil

1 tablespoon soy sauce

¼ teaspoon kosher salt

¼ teaspoon freshly ground black pepper

1. Soak the glutinous rice in water for 4 hours or overnight.

2. When you're ready to cook, drain and rinse the rice. Slice the kabocha into 1-inch-thick slices. Discard seeds and stem.

3. Prepare a two-tiered metal steamer **(see page 35),** use two steamers, or steam in two batches. Place a 1-inch-thick layer of the rice in a shallow heatproof bowl that will fit into your steamer. Bring the water to a boil, cover, and steam the rice and kabocha slices over medium-high heat for 20 minutes or until the rice is translucent, soft, and chewy and the kabocha is soft but retains its shape. When the squash is cool enough to handle, peel it with a small knife and cut the slices crosswise into ¼-inch-thick pieces.

4. **Meanwhile, make the Brussels sprouts:** Heat the oven to 425°F. Toss the Brussels sprouts with the olive oil, soy sauce, salt, and pepper. Bake for 15 minutes or until crispy. Set aside and keep warm.

5. **Make the risotto:** Heat the olive oil in a medium saucepan over medium-low heat. Add the onion and garlic and cook until softened, 6 to 8 minutes.

6. Add the water and cook until it evaporates and the onion is completely soft and translucent but not browned, 8 to 10 minutes.

7. Stir in the glutinous rice, kabocha, and wine. Reduce the heat to low and cook, stirring constantly, until the wine has evaporated, about 2 minutes.

8. Stir in the stock in ½-cup increments, allowing each to be absorbed before adding the next. This should take 15 to 20 minutes total. The kabocha and rice will have continued to break down.

9. Remove from the heat. Gradually mix in the butter and Parmesan until they are melted and the risotto is creamy.

10. Season with salt and pepper to taste, top with the Brussels sprouts, and serve.

**SUBSTITUTE:** You can substitute Honeynut, delicata, or butternut squash for the kabocha; you don't need to steam them.

# PORK AND TOFU MEATBALL SOUP WITH ASPARAGUS AND DILL

Serves 4; makes 12 meatballs

**When you're making meatballs, texture is as important as flavor. The size of the ingredients also matters. Here, instead of adding chopped scallions, I blitz them in water first so they are incorporated into the meat smoothly. Silken tofu helps make the meatballs incredibly tender. They're cooked by the gentle process of poaching, which keeps them intact. With its garlicky broth, fresh dill, fennel, peas, and asparagus, this is a very refreshing spring bowl.**

1. **Make the ginger-scallion water:** Combine the water, scallions, and ginger in a blender and blitz until smooth. Strain through a fine-mesh sieve, reserving the liquid and discarding any solids.

2. **Make the meatballs:** Mix 2 tablespoons of the ginger-scallion water, the ground pork, silken tofu, garlic, soy sauce, Shaoxing wine, salt, and black pepper in a medium bowl. Stir in one direction until the mixture is sticky. Place in the fridge to chill for 15 to 20 minutes.

3. **Meanwhile, make the soup:** Heat the olive oil in a large saucepan over medium heat. Add the fennel, season with the salt, and cook until softened and translucent, 6 to 8 minutes.

4. Add the ginger and garlic and cook for 30 seconds or until fragrant. Add the stock, bring to a gentle boil, then reduce the heat to medium-low to maintain a gentle simmer. Add the fish sauce, then season with more salt to taste, if needed.

5. Scoop out 1 heaping tablespoon of the meatball mixture at a time, roll between your palms, then gently place it in the stock, making 12 meatballs. Reduce the heat to low and poach for 10 minutes or until the meatballs are cooked through and float.

6. Add the asparagus and peas and cook until bright green and tender, about 3 minutes.

7. Divide between the bowls. Top with the dill, scallions, a sprinkle of white pepper, and a squeeze of lemon juice, and serve.

## PORK AND TOFU MEATBALLS

8 ounces (225 g) ground pork, preferably not lean

4 ounces (115 g) silken tofu (about ½ cup)

1 garlic clove, grated

1 tablespoon soy sauce

1 tablespoon Shaoxing wine

¾ teaspoon kosher salt

½ teaspoon ground black pepper

## SOUP

2 tablespoons extra-virgin olive oil

1 medium bulb fennel, cored and diced (1½ cups)

1 teaspoon kosher salt, plus more

Two ¼-inch-thick slices ginger

3 garlic cloves, peeled and smashed

4 cups (960 g) unsalted chicken stock

1 tablespoon fish sauce

1 cup 1-inch pieces asparagus (about 6 spears/110 g)

1 cup (165 g) frozen green peas

¼ cup (9 g) chopped fresh dill

2 scallions, trimmed and thinly sliced

Ground white pepper

Lemon wedges

## GINGER-SCALLION WATER

1 cup water

2 scallions, trimmed

One ¼-inch-thick slice ginger

Combine the water, scallions, and ginger in a blender and blitz until smooth. Strain through a fine-mesh sieve, reserving the liquid and discarding any solids.

# COD IN SPICED TOMATO BROTH WITH RICE

Serves 4

**I love soupy rice—泡饭 *pào fàn*—in which cooked (usually leftover) rice is added to a hot soup and turned into something comforting and delicious. In this variation on the classic, poaching boneless white fish in a flavorful base allows the essence of the poaching liquid to seep into the fish. Add rice or any other cooked grain to the broth before serving, and you've got a good, quick weeknight meal.**

2 teaspoons kosher salt, plus more to taste

2 teaspoons sugar, divided

1 pound (455 g) skinless cod fillet, or another firm, white fish fillet like haddock, cut into 4 pieces

1 tablespoon Shaoxing wine

2 tablespoons neutral oil, such as canola or grapeseed

4 garlic cloves, minced

1 teaspoon minced peeled ginger

3 scallions, trimmed, white parts minced, green parts thinly sliced

1 teaspoon red pepper flakes

1 teaspoon smoked paprika

1 can (28 ounces/794 g) crushed tomatoes

3 cups (720 g) unsalted chicken or vegetable stock

1 tablespoon light soy sauce

Freshly ground black pepper

About 2 cups (400 g) cooked white rice

Cilantro sprigs

Lemon wedges

1. Combine the salt and 1 teaspoon of the sugar in a small bowl. Sprinkle over the fish and let cure for 15 minutes in the refrigerator.

2. Rinse the fish, pat dry, then brush with the Shaoxing wine.

3. Heat the oil in a medium saucepan over medium heat. Add the garlic, ginger, and the white parts of scallions and cook until fragrant and golden, about 2 minutes. Add the red pepper flakes and smoked paprika and toast for another minute, until fragrant.

4. Add the tomatoes and their juices and cook until the liquid is reduced, about 7 minutes.

5. Add the stock, soy sauce, and remaining 1 teaspoon sugar and stir to combine. Cook for about another 10 minutes, stirring occasionally, until the broth has thickened. Season to taste with salt and black pepper.

6. Bring to a bubbling simmer over medium heat, then gently lay the fish pieces in the broth. Immediately cover tightly, turn the heat to the lowest setting, and let sit until the fish is just cooked, 6 to 8 minutes depending on the thickness of the fillets. To make sure the white flesh is opaque, use a chopstick to flake off a piece.

7. Divide the cooked rice between bowls. Carefully ladle a piece of cod and some tomato broth over the rice. Top with cilantro, the scallion greens, and a squeeze of lemon and serve.

**SUBSTITUTE:** You can use grains other than white rice with this dish: farro, barley, brown rice, or wild rice are all wonderful options.

# WATERCRESS CONGEE WITH MARINATED MUSHROOMS

Serves 4

**Congee, also known as *zhou*, *jook*, or *juk*, is defined by its texture and toppings. The most basic form is just rice and water. The rice grains are broken down through the simmering process, with the released starch contributing to the consistency of the congee. Freezing the rice is a shortcut. It causes the moisture in the grains to expand, which starts to break them up, accelerating the congee cooking process. In this dish, seared mushrooms are marinated in vinegar, and a bright watercress puree brings spunkiness.**

1. Rinse the raw rice until the water runs clear, then drain. Place in a freezer-safe container and freeze overnight.

2. Combine the rice vinegar, sugar, and soy sauce in a medium bowl.

3. Heat 1 tablespoon of the olive oil in a medium saucepan over medium-high heat until it shimmers. Add the mushroom slices and sauté until golden and crispy, 5 to 7 minutes. Transfer to the bowl with the vinegar–soy sauce mixture.

4. In the same saucepan, bring 6 cups of the stock to a boil. Add the frozen rice and bring back to a boil, stirring often to prevent sticking.

5. Reduce the heat to low and simmer for 20 to 25 minutes, stirring occasionally, until the rice begins to break down and fall apart.

6. Check the texture: at this point, it should be the consistency of porridge. If you want a thinner congee, add more water or stock. If you want a thicker texture, cook the congee longer to reduce the liquid.

7. While the congee cooks, bring a separate medium pot of salted water to a boil and prepare an ice water bath. Blanch the watercress for 30 to 60 seconds, until bright green, then place in the water bath to stop the cooking.

8. Drain the watercress well and gently wring to squeeze out water. Place in a blender with the remaining ¼ cup stock, the garlic cloves, and the remaining 2 tablespoons olive oil. Blitz until smooth. Season with the kosher salt and ¼ teaspoon white pepper. Keep the remaining puree in the fridge and use as a topping or incorporate into sauces.

9. Divide the congee between four bowls, then top each bowl with a tablespoon of watercress puree. Divide the marinated mushrooms between the bowls.

10. Top with the scallion, a drizzle of chile crisp, a sprinkle of flaky salt, and more white pepper, and serve.

¾ cup (160 g) raw short-grain white rice or 2 cups (340 g) cooked white rice

1 tablespoon rice vinegar

2 teaspoons sugar

1 teaspoon light soy sauce

3 tablespoons extra-virgin olive oil, divided

8 ounces (225 g) king oyster mushrooms (about 4 medium), thinly sliced lengthwise

6¼ to 8¼ cups (1500 to 1980 g) water or unsalted chicken or vegetable stock, divided

10 ounces (300 g) watercress (about 1½ bunches)

3 garlic cloves, peeled and smashed

1 teaspoon kosher salt

Ground white pepper

1 scallion, trimmed and thinly sliced

**Fried Shallot Chile Crisp (page 207)** or store-bought chile crisp

Flaky salt

**SUBSTITUTE:** If you can't get oyster mushrooms, fleshy mushrooms like shiitakes or maitakes work well, too. Button mushrooms are still more fleshy; if this is the only mushroom you can find, slice them very thin.

# SAVORY MISO OATS

Serves 2

I've been making this dish regularly for years. It's a sister to congee. I came upon the creamy yet slightly crispy mix of old-fashioned rolled oats and steel-cut oats in April Bloomfield's *A Girl and Her Pig,* and I've used the combination ever since. If you want to increase the serving size, the ratio is 1 part combined oats to 3 parts water, by volume. The oats are flavored with white (shiro) miso and a touch of soy sauce, then topped with a runny poached egg and furikake seasoning. A great weeknight meal.

3 cups (720 g) water, plus more as needed

2 tablespoons (36 g) white (shiro) miso

1 teaspoon soy sauce

½ cup (70 g) old-fashioned rolled oats

½ cup (95 g) steel-cut oats

2 large eggs

Nori furikake **(see Notes)**

**Fried Shallot Chile Crisp (page 207)** or store-bought chile crisp

Flaky salt and freshly ground black pepper

1. Bring the water to a boil in a small saucepan. Dissolve the miso in the water, then add the soy sauce. Add the rolled oats and steel-cut oats and stir. Reduce the heat to low and simmer uncovered, stirring often, until the water has been absorbed and the oats are tender but still chewy, 15 to 20 minutes. Add a bit more water if it has all been absorbed before the oats are tender.

2. **Poach the eggs:** While the oats are cooking, crack the eggs into individual ramekins. Fill a saucepan with water and bring to a boil, then reduce the heat to maintain a gentle simmer. Use a wooden spoon to create a gentle whirl—you should see a vortex. Gently slide each egg in, one at a time. They will spin with the vortex. Turn off the heat, cover with the lid, and let sit for 3½ minutes. Remove with a slotted spoon and drain on a paper towel–lined plate.

3. Divide the oats among two bowls. Top each with a poached egg, followed by a sprinkle of furikake, a drizzle of chile crisp, and flaky salt and freshly ground black pepper.

**NOTE:** Furikake seasoning is a Japanese rice seasoning that is usually savory and sweet, made from a mixture of sesame seeds, dried nori, and a variety of other umami contributors such as dried fish flakes. Many varieties are sold in most Asian grocery stores as well as in many Western supermarkets. I always keep some on hand for an instant crunchy, flavorful topping. You can substitute toasted sesame seeds or flaked dried seaweed.

# SAFFRON POACHED CHICKEN

Serves 2 to 4

**Poaching is used frequently to cook chicken in Chinese cuisine since it keeps the meat succulent and tender, and as a bonus, yields a flavorful broth to serve with the bird. Here, I poach whole chicken legs in a saffron-tinted liquid, lending them a beautiful color and fragrance and enhancing the intrinsic flavor. This method keeps the meat juicy with minimal fuss. As with any chicken dish, make sure the interior reaches 165°F. I insert a chopstick into the thick part of the thigh; if the juices run clear, it is ready. (You can also use a meat thermometer.) This dish is fantastic served simply, with a scoop of rice.**

1. Bring a large saucepan of water to a boil over high heat.

2. Add the ginger, saffron, Shaoxing wine, and ½ teaspoon of the salt, reduce the heat to low, and simmer for 10 minutes.

3. Add the chicken legs. Add a bit more water if needed to completely submerge them. Increase the heat and bring to a boil. Then reduce the heat to the lowest setting so the liquid is at a tiny gurgling simmer, and cover tightly. Poach for 10 minutes.

4. Turn off the heat, keeping the pot tightly covered, and let sit for another 20 minutes. Meanwhile, set up an ice water bath.

5. Remove the chicken from the saucepan and immediately place in the water bath. Let sit for 10 minutes.

6. While the chicken is cooling, strain the stock. Clean out the saucepan and return the stock to it. Bring to a simmer over medium-high heat and cook until reduced by half, about 15 minutes. Season with the remaining 1 teaspoon salt and white pepper to taste.

7. At this point, you can leave the legs whole or chop them with a cleaver or butcher knife, leaving the drumsticks whole and cutting the thighs into 1½-inch segments.

8. Divide the chicken between two bowls and pour the saffron-chicken stock over them.

9. Top with a sprinkle of scallion and a drizzle of sesame oil and serve.

Four ⅛-inch-thick slices ginger

½ teaspoon saffron threads

2 tablespoons Shaoxing wine

1½ teaspoons kosher salt, divided

2 chicken leg quarters, including thighs (1½ pounds/680 g total)

Ground white pepper

1 scallion, trimmed and minced

Toasted sesame oil

**SUBSTITUTE:** You can use this method for a small whole chicken (about 2½ pounds/ 1135 g). After bringing the water to a boil in step 3, dunk the chicken in it 2 or 3 times so the water runs throughout the inner cavity; this helps the bird cook evenly. Then place the chicken in the water, reduce the heat to low, cover, and poach for 12 minutes. In step 4, let sit for 30 minutes instead of 20.

# GREEN BEANS AND BUTTER BEANS IN HERBED SOY-VINEGAR SAUCE

Serves 4

**This dish uses both boiling and saucing techniques. Blanched green beans are the star here, tender yet still crunchy and juicy. There are a few ways to season cooked green vegetables: drizzle, 淋味 *lín wèi*; toss to coat, 拌味 *bàn wèi*; or serve on the side like a dip, 沾味 *zhān wèi*. Here, I toss the beans in the marinade to steep (拌味 *bàn wèi*), like a salad. Butter beans are the ultimate vehicles for absorbing flavor.**

½ cup (20 g) finely chopped mixed fresh dill and parsley

¼ cup (60 g) extra-virgin olive oil

2 garlic cloves, grated

1 teaspoon soy sauce

1 teaspoon black vinegar

1 teaspoon rice vinegar

1 teaspoon sugar

¼ teaspoon red pepper flakes

Freshly ground black pepper

1 can (15.5 ounces/439 g) butter beans, rinsed and drained

½ medium red onion, finely diced (¾ cup/100 g)

Kosher salt

½ teaspoon toasted sesame oil

1 pound (455 g) green beans, ends trimmed

Freshly squeezed lemon juice

2 scallions, trimmed and thinly sliced

1. Mix together the herbs, olive oil, garlic, soy sauce, black vinegar, rice vinegar, sugar, red pepper flakes, and a few grinds of black pepper in a large bowl.

2. Toss the butter beans and red onion with the sauce and let sit while you blanch the green beans.

3. Bring a large pot of salted water to a boil. Add the sesame oil, then the green beans, and blanch for 90 seconds or until bright green but still crunchy. Drain and rinse with cold water until they're cooled slightly but still warm.

4. Toss the warm green beans with the butter beans. Season to taste with salt, black pepper, and lemon juice. Stir in the scallions and serve.

**NOTE:** You can chop the green beans into bite-sized pieces or keep them longer.

**SUBSTITUTE:** Cannellini beans, navy beans, or black-eyed peas can be used in place of the butter beans.

# JIŬ NIÀNG POACHED PEARS

Serves 4

**For this punchy, floral, fruity dessert soup, Asian pears are poached in water and fermented rice wine, called 酒酿 *jiŭ niàng*. It's made by fermenting sweet glutinous rice with a specific distiller's yeast, creating a sweet, yeasty liquid that contains grains of the fermented rice. It's believed to boost milk production in postpartum women, and after I had my son, my mom made me *jiŭ niàng* soup every day. I'm not sure if it helped, but it was certainly delicious!**

1. Combine the water, wine and its fermented rice, brown sugar, and orange peel in a medium saucepan. Bring to a boil, then reduce the heat to low and simmer for 5 minutes or until the brown sugar dissolves completely.

2. Add the pear halves; the liquid should just cover the pears.

3. Bring back to a boil, then reduce the heat to low and simmer gently, uncovered, for 1 hour or until a fork pierces the flesh easily.

4. Divide among four bowls, allotting one pear half per bowl, and serve.

4 cups (960 g) water

½ cup (120 g) *jiŭ niàng* (fermented rice wine)

2 tablespoons dark brown sugar

2 strips orange peel (avoid the white pith)

2 Asian pears, peeled, halved, and cored

# 炖

*dùn*

# BRAISE

Braising involves cooking food partially submerged in liquid in a heat-retaining vessel, usually covered, over low heat. Maintaining even heat is important so that the liquid stays at a constant low-level bubble—a simmer, not a rolling boil. It's similar to Western-style braising, except that the Chinese way usually starts by parboiling the meat—and even tofu—in water, to cleanse it and remove any impurities, which rise to the top as scum.

Although we're inclined to think of braising as taking hours, in fact, the timing depends on the ingredient. The famous braise mapo tofu, for example, is ready fairly quickly, because tofu requires less time to cook than meat. Vegetables are also fairly quick-cooking. Meats, on the other hand, need time for their connective tissues to soften and the flavors of the braising liquid to seep in. Lamb shanks, beef short ribs, and other tough cuts are rich in collagen, which melts into gelatin, thickening the braising liquid, while braises with tofu and vegetables may benefit from the addition of starch to thicken them. Because of their abundant gravy, braises are delightful served with rice or over noodles.

Like the other cooking techniques we've looked at, braising divides into subcategories, depending on the intensity of the heat used, the vessel being braised in, the duration of cooking, the amount of liquid, and the flavors in the braising liquid. Though what follows is by no means a comprehensive list, the braises I describe here are those commonly used in home cooking.

## 红烧 RED-BRAISE *hóng shāo*

Red-braising is the braising method of Shanghai. The term refers to the elixir of Shaoxing wine, soy sauce, aromatics, and sugar that makes up the braising liquid, which cooks down into a succulent, fragrant, thick, glossy glaze. This classic flavor profile evokes a world of memories for me, as this is the braising method I grew up with. In a classic Shanghai red braise, the ingredient (typically meat) is often browned in a mixture of oil and caramelized sugar, a step that heightens its redness, before the braising liquid is added. Fish, pork, beef, tofu, and egg can all be red-braised. Red-braising also brings out the intrinsic sweetness and meatiness of kabocha squash (**page 137**).

## 红烧 WHITE- OR CLEAR-BRAISE 白烧 *bái shāo*

This method replaces most of the soy sauce with stock and wine, while keeping the aromatic seasonings and sugar. The treatment is especially good for duck, because it allows its distinctive flavor to shine.

## 红烧 STEAM-BRAISE 焖 *mèn*

In a steam-braise, the cooking is done in a tightly covered heat-retaining pot. In **Dōng Pō Ròu (page 133),** for example, cubes of pork belly steam-braise in a tightly closed pot, becoming impossibly fragrant. The flavors may seem similar to those of a red braise, but the recipe omits the browning in oil and sugar in favor of steaming in Shaoxing rice wine. This technique is also used for large chunks of meat like lamb shanks that need a long cooking time, since cocooning everything in the pot makes for flavor-concentrated, tender results.

## STEW 炖 *dùn*

Falling between braising and boiling, this gentle, gradually simmered braise contains more liquid than a typical braise but is kept at a temperature well below a boil. The goal is not a dish with a thick, gravy-like sauce, but one that incorporates the braising liquid as an integral part of the dish. It is less soy sauce–based and more stock-based.

## STEEP-BRAISE 卤 *lǔ*

This form of braising infuses even more flavors from the liquid into the food by letting it steep in it after it's braised. A classic example is the marbled tea egg, where cooked eggs are braised in a soy sauce and tea mixture, then left to drink up more flavor. I've included a different interpretation, braised quail eggs.

# DŌNG PŌ RÒU

东坡肉 | *dōng pō ròu* | Serves 4

***Dōng pō ròu*** 东坡肉 is a famous red-cooked pork belly dish from Hangzhou, a city near Shanghai.

It is luscious—boldly flavored, salty, yet sweet, and rich, with a generous amount of fat that doesn't taste fatty. It's named after the celebrated artist, Su DongPo, an eleventh-century poet, writer, and calligrapher. The pork belly is steam-braised in a rich mixture of soy sauce, rice wine, and sugar. Its presentation is no less gorgeous: cut into generous cubes, it's served in a clay pot, the vessel in which it is cooked. It's a beautiful dish. Given its complex flavor, you'd expect this dish to be quite complicated—but it's actually easy once you have things all set up. You leave it to braise, then steam in its clay pot (or any vessel). In the process, the pork belly becomes so melting-

1. To parboil the pork belly, put enough water to submerge it in a large pot. Add 1 tablespoon of the Shaoxing wine and bring to a boil. Add the pork belly. Bring the water back to a boil and let boil for 1 minute. Drain the pork belly and discard the liquid.

2. When the pork is cool enough to handle, cut it into four 2½- to 3-inch squares.

3. Line a medium clay pot or heavy-bottomed saucepan large enough to fit all four squares in a single layer with the scallions. Place the ginger slices over the scallions. Place the pork belly, skin side down, on top of the aromatics.

4. Combine the remaining 2 cups (480 g) Shaoxing wine, light soy sauce, and dark soy sauce in a small bowl. Pour into the pot. The liquid should come half to three-quarters of the way up the pork belly. Add water if necessary. Sprinkle the rock sugar over the pork belly.

5. Bring to a boil, then reduce the heat to the lowest setting. Cover and simmer for 1½ hours or until the cubes are deep brown and the rock sugar has dissolved. At this point, the cubes will be wobbly but not fork-tender.

6. Use tongs to gently turn the pork belly skin side up, cover again, and simmer for another 1½ hours or until meltingly tender—a chopstick inserted should easily slide in.

7. At this point, you can place the pot in the fridge to let the fat solidify, then skim it off. Or you can just use a spoon to skim off as much surface fat from the hot liquid as you can.

8. After removing the fat, slowly increase the heat to high and boil the braising liquid until it is thickened and reduced by half, about 20 minutes. The liquid will have small foam-like bubbles, not big boiling water–type bubbles. If the pork belly cubes are starting to fall apart, gently remove them and set aside.

9. Serve hot, with some of the braising liquid spooned over the pork belly.

2 cups plus 1 tablespoon (495 g) Shaoxing wine, divided

2 pounds (910 g) skin-on fatty boneless pork belly

6 scallions, trimmed

Three ¼-inch-thick slices ginger

¼ cup (60 g) light soy sauce

2 teaspoons dark soy sauce

5 ounces (140 g) rock sugar, crushed slightly with a mortar and pestle (some large chunks remaining are fine; about ⅔ cup)

**NOTES:** *Dōng pō ròu* is one of two red-cooked pork dishes from the Jiangnan region in southeastern China. The other is the well-known Shanghainese *hóng shāo ròu* (red-braised pork belly), which has a similar flavor profile. In that dish, the pork belly is first fried in caramel, and the meat is cut into smaller pieces. (That recipe is in my book *My Shanghai*.)

The pork belly for this recipe should have the skin (rind) on and visible layers of fat and meat. In Asian grocery stores, it's usually sold in 1½- to 2-inch-thick strips and labeled 五花肉 *wǔ huā ròu*, meaning five layers. In American butcher shops, I have seen larger slabs. Either works.

# MAPO TOFU

麻婆豆腐 | *má pó dòu fu* | Serves 4

**The popularity of mapo tofu has shot up in the past few years—and with good reason! It's a dish that hits all the right notes: spicy, umami, saucy, with a luxurious mouthfeel. Cubes of soft tofu are braised in a rich liquid, with fermented broad bean paste and ground pork melding together to achieve the umami. It's excellent paired with rice—in fact, I insist on this!**

1 pound (455 g) soft tofu

1½ teaspoons coarsely ground red Sichuan peppercorns, divided

1 teaspoon red pepper flakes

6 tablespoons neutral oil, such as canola or grapeseed, divided

4 or 5 dried red Sichuan chile peppers, stemmed and roughly chopped

½ teaspoon fennel seeds

1 piece cassia bark or cinnamon stick

2 garlic cloves, minced

1 teaspoon minced peeled ginger

8 ounces (225 g) ground pork

2 tablespoons doubanjiang (fermented broad bean paste)

⅔ cup (170 g) unsalted chicken stock, or whatever stock you have, or water

1 tablespoon cornstarch mixed with 2 tablespoons water

½ teaspoon ground white pepper

Cooked white rice

1 scallion, trimmed and finely chopped

1. Gently cut the soft tofu into ½- to ¾-inch cubes.

2. Bring a medium saucepan of water to a boil, then add the soft tofu. Reduce the heat to low and boil for 30 to 60 seconds, then carefully remove the tofu with a slotted spoon and drain on a paper towel–lined plate.

3. To make a quick chile oil, heat a wok over low heat. Place ½ teaspoon of the ground Sichuan peppercorns and the red pepper flakes in a medium bowl. Add ¼ cup (60 g) of the oil to the wok and heat until tiny bubbles form around a wooden chopstick when you stick it in the oil. Add the dried chile peppers, fennel seeds, and cassia or cinnamon and stir-fry until fragrant, about 2 minutes. Make sure not to burn the peppers. Pour the oil and spices into the bowl with the red pepper flakes and set aside.

4. Return the wok to the heat and add the remaining 2 tablespoons oil. Add the garlic and ginger and stir-fry until fragrant, about 30 seconds. Add the ground pork and stir-fry until browned, 6 to 7 minutes, breaking it up into small crumbles as it cooks.

5. Add the remaining 1 teaspoon ground Sichuan peppercorns and the doubanjiang to the pork and stir-fry to combine. Add the stock and stir to incorporate. Bring to a boil, reduce the heat to low, and let simmer and gently bubble for 5 minutes or until the sauce has begun to thicken.

6. Stir in the cornstarch slurry, reserved chile oil, and white pepper and mix to combine. Add the tofu cubes and stir very gently to combine by tracing around the circumference of the wok with the back of a spoon. Simmer for 5 to 10 minutes, until the sauce has thickened to a gravy-like consistency—it should coat the back of your spoon. Serve with rice, topped with the scallion.

**A NOTE ON HEAT:** Spiciness is highly subjective. My advice is to keep sampling the braising liquid to judge the spice level. If your tolerance is low, start with just 1 tablespoon of the fermented broad bean paste and half the chile peppers and peppercorns, and go from there.

# RED-BRAISED KABOCHA SQUASH

Serves 4

Come autumn, I, like many other West-to-East-Coast transplants, rush to the store for the gorgeous varieties of squash: delicata, honeynut, acorn, kabocha. The sturdy, squat kabocha squash is a favorite of mine—its thick skin hides an earthy, sweet orange flesh. In this recipe, wedges of kabocha are cooked with the traditional 红烧 *hóng shāo*, red-braise method: the squash is browned in hot melted sugar, then braised in a liquid seasoned with soy sauce, sugar, and rice wine.

1. Heat the oil in a wok or large heavy-bottomed skillet over low heat. Sprinkle in 1 tablespoon of the crushed rock sugar and stir to dissolve.

2. Working in batches, lay the kabocha wedges, cut side down, in the sugary oil in a single layer and cook undisturbed until browned, 6 to 8 minutes. Turn and brown the other side. Transfer the kabocha to a plate.

3. Add a splash of oil if the pan is dry, and add the shiitake mushrooms and cremini mushrooms. Stir-fry until browned, about 6 minutes, then transfer to a small bowl.

4. Add another splash of oil if the pan is dry, and add the scallions, ginger, and garlic and stir-fry until fragrant, about 1 minute.

5. Return the kabocha to the pan and arrange in one layer. Add the water, Shaoxing wine, light soy sauce, dark soy sauce, the remaining 1 tablespoon rock sugar, and the star anise. The liquid should come halfway up the wedges; add a bit more water if necessary. Bring to a boil, then reduce the heat to medium-low. Cover partially with a lid and simmer gently until the squash is tender but not falling apart, 8 to 10 minutes.

6. Uncover and turn the squash pieces. If the squash is already fully tender, carefully remove it from the pan and set aside. Add the mushrooms to the braising liquid. Cover, and cook for another 3 minutes, until the squash is tender or the liquid has thickened.

7. Increase the heat to high and cook until the liquid has reduced by half, about 5 minutes. Gently stir in the cornstarch slurry and cook until the liquid reaches a gravy-like consistency, coating the back of a spoon, 1 to 2 minutes.

8. Add the butter and stir gently to create a silky sauce. Return the kabocha wedges to the sauce, garnish with the sliced scallion (if using), and serve.

2 tablespoons neutral oil

2 tablespoons coarsely crushed rock sugar, divided

1½ pounds (680 g) kabocha squash (about 1 small), washed well, seeded, and cut into 2-inch-thick wedges

4 ounces (115 g) fresh shiitake mushrooms, stemmed and halved

4 ounces (115 g) cremini mushrooms, stemmed and halved

4 scallions, trimmed and roughly chopped

Two ¼-inch-thick slices ginger

2 garlic cloves, peeled and smashed

1½ cups (360 g) water, plus more as necessary

2 tablespoons Shaoxing wine

2 tablespoons light soy sauce

1 teaspoon dark soy sauce

1 piece star anise

1 teaspoon cornstarch mixed with 1 tablespoon water

2 tablespoons unsalted butter

1 scallion, trimmed and thinly sliced crosswise (optional)

**NOTE:** Make sure to cut the kabocha wedges of equal thickness so they cook evenly.

**SUBSTITUTE:** If you can't find kabocha, you can use other squashes—just remember some squash will be done sooner than others. Delicata, for example, is thinner and will cook more quickly.

# MISO-BRAISED EGGS WITH SHALLOTS

Serves 4

This dish stars hard-cooked eggs in a sweet and tangy miso braising liquid. I love how simple yet full of flavor it is. It was inspired by my go-to comfort food when I was growing up, red-braised pork belly, in which the eggs that were always included were a favorite and divided quickly among us. The eggs are fried in oil so they get a golden crust, then are braised in a mixture of miso and shallots, which in turn become buttery soft. Instead of the soy sauce–rich braising liquid that characterizes a red braise, I use a heady mix of miso, tangy black vinegar, sweet and jammy shallots, and just a touch of soy as the base for the braise.

8 large eggs

1 cup (240 g) water

2 tablespoons white (shiro) miso

1 tablespoon black vinegar, plus more as needed

1 tablespoon maple syrup

1 teaspoon light soy sauce

2 tablespoons neutral oil, such as canola or grapeseed, plus more as needed

8 medium shallots (about 1 pound/455 g total), peeled and halved **(see Note)**

4 tablespoons (½ stick; 115 g) unsalted butter, cut into small pieces

Flaky salt

1. Place the eggs in a saucepan large enough to fit them in a single layer and cover with cold water by 1 inch. Bring to a boil, then reduce the heat to medium-low and simmer (do not boil) for 8 minutes. Meanwhile, prepare an ice water bath.

2. After exactly 8 minutes, transfer the eggs to the water bath. While the eggs cool, whisk together the water, miso, black vinegar, maple syrup, and soy sauce and set aside.

3. Heat the oil in a wok or Dutch oven over medium heat until it shimmers. Add the shallots, cut side down, and let them brown deeply, 7 to 9 minutes. Transfer with a slotted spoon to a plate.

4. When the eggs are cold, peel them. Pat dry with a paper towel.

5. If the pan is dry, add another splash of oil. Place the whole eggs in the shallot oil and fry, stirring gently and often, until they are golden brown and blistered all over, about 2 minutes. (It is OK if they are not completely uniform, given their round contours.) Transfer the eggs to a bowl.

6. Cut two or three slits down the length of each egg, stopping just before you reach the yolk. Return the eggs and shallots to the pan and add the miso braising liquid. It should come halfway up the eggs; add a little more water if needed. Add the butter. Bring to a boil, then reduce the heat to low. Cover and simmer over low heat until the shallots are tender and the liquid has reduced to a gravy-like consistency (it should coat the back of a spoon), about 20 minutes.

7. Uncover and continue braising, stirring and turning the eggs occasionally, until the liquid has reduced further, 10 to 15 minutes.

8. Add a splash of black vinegar, remove from the heat, and stir. Serve immediately, with a generous sprinkle of flaky salt.

**NOTE:** Try to keep a bit of the root end intact so the shallots hold together.

# WINE-BRAISED DUCK LEGS WITH BEANS

Serves 2

**Duck legs are simmered in Shaoxing wine and stock, a clear braise that keeps their lightly gamey taste at the forefront while adding delicate hints of the rice wine. First the duck is cured overnight with salt—this step not only seasons the meat but also keeps it tender and juicy, while simultaneously drying the skin so you get maximum crispiness when it's browned. Then it's braised on the stovetop until the meat is so tender that it nearly falls off the bone. It will get a final quick pan-sear to crisp it up again before being placed on the beans, which have soaked up the aromatic braising liquid.**

1. Pat the duck dry, then salt it all over. Let sit in the fridge uncovered for 2 hours or overnight, skin side up.

2. Rinse the duck and pat dry. Trim off any excess fat. Place the duck, skin side down, in a Dutch oven or deep skillet over medium-high heat. Sear for 3 minutes.

3. Turn the heat down to medium-low and continue to sear the duck and let the fat render. Press down firmly with a spatula or use a weight, if necessary, to ensure even contact with the pan. Sear until the skin easily lifts from the pan and is golden brown, 6 to 8 minutes.

4. Flip and sear the flesh side for 1 to 2 minutes, until browned. Transfer the duck legs to a plate.

5. Pour off all but 2 tablespoons fat from the pan. Add the 4 roughly chopped scallions and the ginger and briefly stir-fry. Return the duck to the pan, skin side up. Add the stock, Shaoxing wine, soy sauce, mandarin orange peel, star anise, rock sugar, and white pepper. The braising liquid should come halfway up the duck legs. Add more stock if needed.

6. Bring to a boil, reduce the heat to the lowest setting, and braise, partially covered, for 1½ hours. The liquid should gently bubble.

7. Remove the lid and let cook for another hour, until the duck is fork-tender and easily comes apart.

8. Remove the duck from the pan and set aside. Using a slotted spoon, remove the scallions and other aromatics from the braising liquid and discard.

9. Add the beans to the braising liquid and simmer for about 10 minutes, until it has thickened.

10. Meanwhile, heat a large nonstick skillet over medium heat. Add the duck legs skin side down, and crisp the skin, 3 to 5 minutes.

11. Remove the beans from the heat and add a splash of balsamic vinegar. Stir to combine.

12. Divide the beans between two plates, including the gravy. Dollop each serving with 1 tablespoon of the crème fraîche and place a duck leg quarter on top. Garnish with the finely chopped scallion and serve immediately.

---

2 duck leg quarters (leg and thigh)

1 tablespoon kosher salt

5 scallions, trimmed; 4 roughly chopped, 1 finely chopped

Three ¼-inch-thick slices ginger

1¼ cups (300 g) unsalted chicken stock or whatever stock you have, plus more as needed

½ cup (120 g) Shaoxing wine

2 tablespoons light soy sauce

2 strips dried mandarin orange peel

1 piece star anise

1 tablespoon crushed rock sugar

¼ teaspoon ground white pepper

1 can (15.5 ounces/439 g) cannellini or butter beans, drained and rinsed (1½ cups)

Balsamic vinegar

2 tablespoons crème fraîche

**NOTE:** Be sure to save the rendered duck fat—use a dab of it along with oil for frying for an additional boost of flavor.

# GOCHUJANG-BRAISED EGGPLANT

Serves 4

**Steaming eggplant is my favorite way to transform its texture from spongy to creamy, without making it oily as frying does. This recipe is based on the traditional technique for making vegetarian unagi (eel). The eggplant is first steamed until it's three-quarters cooked. Then it's splayed open, browned on a pan, and braised in a rich gochujang-flavored braising liquid, until the flavor has seeped into the eggplant and the liquid thickens, coating it. Serve over white rice.**

Two 12-ounces (350 g) Chinese or Japanese eggplants

⅔ cup (160 g) water

2 tablespoons gochujang

1 tablespoon light soy sauce

1 tablespoon honey

2 teaspoons apple cider vinegar

2 tablespoons neutral oil, such as canola or grapeseed

3 garlic cloves, minced

Lemon wedges

Toasted sesame seeds

1 scallion, trimmed and finely chopped

1. Trim the stem from each eggplant. Cut the eggplants in half crosswise, then cut each half lengthwise, for four pieces per eggplant.

2. Prepare a steamer **(see page 35).** Place the eggplant pieces in the steamer and steam over high heat for about 6 minutes. The eggplant should be fork-tender but not so cooked through that the flesh collapses. Set aside to cool slightly.

3. Mix the water, soy, gochujang, honey, and vinegar in a small bowl and set aside.

4. Place the pieces of eggplant skin side down on a cutting board. Use a sharp knife to cut 8-millimeter-long slits lengthwise along the cut side, stopping halfway deep into the eggplant so it stays together. Angle your knife and make crosshatch marks, also stopping halfway through the flesh. (Crosshatching makes the eggplant flatter and more rectangular so it sears better.)

5. Heat the oil in a large skillet with a lid or a Dutch oven over medium-high heat. Working in batches if necessary, sear the crosshatched eggplant pieces, cut side down, until browned, 2 to 3 minutes.

6. Add another glug of oil, then add garlic and cook until softened, 1–2 minutes. Return all the pieces to the pan and add the braising liquid. Cover, turn the heat down to low, and simmer for 3 to 5 minutes or until eggplant is tender but still holds its shape and sauce has thickened.

7. Remove the lid and finish the dish with a squeeze of lemon, a sprinkle of toasted sesame seeds, and the scallions.

**NOTE:** Be sure to adjust the braising liquid according to your spice tolerance—you can start with 1 tablespoon gochujang if you know you are spice sensitive.

# BRAISED LAMB SHANKS WITH KIMCHI AND LEEKS

Serves 4

Lamb shanks are hearty cuts with a large bone that are superb when braised. I like to season them with salt and pepper and give them an overnight rest, uncovered, in the fridge. This prep does three things: It allows the flavor to permeate into the meat. The extra flavoring will help season the braising liquid. And the salt also draws moisture out, priming the meat for a good sear; the overnight uncovered rest in the fridge lets the surface dry, leaving a puddle (which is discarded) on the plate.

The braising liquid is supplemented with elements such as kimchi, adding a mild, funky spice, and leeks, with their sweet allium flavor. The leeks are first seared to release their flavors and attain caramelization, then they're added back to the pot later, since they braise much more quickly than the shanks. Served with a side of crisp apple-scallion salad, this makes for a rich meal.

1. **Make the lamb shanks:** Rinse the lamb shanks and pat dry. Season generously with salt and pepper. Let sit in the fridge overnight or for at least 2 hours.

2. Heat the oil in a heavy-bottomed pot large enough to fit the lamb shanks in an even layer over medium-high heat until it shimmers. Add the shanks and brown on all sides, 3 to 5 minutes per side. Transfer the browned shanks to a plate.

3. Sear the leeks, cut sides down, until lightly browned, about 3 minutes. Turn over and sear the side, another 4 minutes. Transfer to the plate with the lamb.

4. Add the onion, garlic, and kimchi and its juices to the pot and sauté until soft, about 10 minutes.

5. Add the brown sugar, gochujang, soy sauce, black vinegar, 1 teaspoon salt, and 1 teaspoon pepper, and stir to coat the vegetables. Return the lamb shanks to the pot and nestle them into the vegetables, then add the Shaoxing wine and stock. Add more stock if needed so that the liquid comes three-quarters of the way up the sides of the meat. Bring to a boil over high heat, then reduce the heat to low, cover, and simmer gently until the meat is fork-tender and easily falls off the bone, 2 to 2 ½ hours.

6. Uncover the pot, place the leeks on top of the lamb shanks, then simmer until the leeks are tender, another 30 minutes.

7. When the leeks are tender, remove the pot from the heat and let sit for 10 minutes.

*Recipe Continues*

## LAMB SHANKS

4 pounds (1820 g) lamb shanks (about 4 shanks), trimmed of excess fat

1 teaspoon kosher salt, plus more to season the lamb

1 teaspoon freshly ground black pepper, plus more to season the lamb

2 tablespoons neutral oil, such as canola or grapeseed

2 medium leeks or 1 large leek (about 1 inch in diameter, 1 pound/455 g), trimmed, cut in half lengthwise, and washed well **(see Note)**

1 large yellow onion, diced (2 cups/330 g)

10 garlic cloves, peeled and smashed

2 cups (about 1 pound/455 g) store-bought napa cabbage kimchi, drained and roughly chopped, juices reserved

*Ingredients Continue*

2 tablespoons brown sugar

2 tablespoons gochujang

2 tablespoons light soy sauce

1 tablespoon black vinegar

½ cup (120 g) Shaoxing wine

3 cups (720 g) unsalted chicken stock or whatever stock you have, plus more as needed

1 tablespoon unsalted butter

## APPLE-SCALLION SALAD

1 crisp medium apple such as Gala, not peeled, cut into matchsticks

2 scallions, trimmed and cut into 2-inch slivers

1 tablespoon rice vinegar

1 teaspoon honey

Kosher salt and freshly ground black pepper

8. With a slotted spoon, remove the lamb and leeks and transfer them to serving plates. Use a large spoon to skim as much fat as you can from the braising liquid. Strain the liquid through a fine-mesh sieve into a bowl and discard the solids. Return the liquid to the pot, bring to a boil over medium-high heat, and reduce by half, 10 to 15 minutes. Stir in the butter.

9. **Meanwhile, make the salad:** Combine the apple and scallions in a large bowl and add the rice vinegar and honey. Toss to combine. Season with salt and pepper to taste.

10. Pour the sauce over the lamb shanks and leeks. Serve with the salad alongside.

**NOTE:** Leeks accumulate dirt in between their leaves and need to be carefully prepped. Rinse well a few times. Trim off the woody outer layer and the root hairs. Cut crosswise or, in this case, lengthwise, exposing the layers. Place the cut parts into a large bowl of cold water and let sit for 10 minutes to allow the grit that's still there to sink to the bottom of the bowl. Rinse a few times and drain thoroughly.

# TOFU WITH SAMBAL AND BURST CHERRY TOMATOES

Serves 2 or 3

Tofu, often incorrectly described as bland, is a great vehicle for bringing flavor to a braise. It comes in varying textures, an indication of its level of hydration. Firmer tofu has gone through a longer pressing step, which extracts moisture from the block. It can stand up to a good sear to give it a golden crust. After that, it's braised in a liquid enriched with jammy cherry tomatoes and the sweet chile paste sambal oelek.

1. Pat the tofu dry with paper towels. Slice the block in half lengthwise so that you have two long rectangles, then slice each rectangle into ½-inch-thick squares. Sprinkle the front and back of the tofu with the cornstarch, so that the tofu is lightly coated with a sticky layer.

2. Stir the sambal oelek, soy sauce, and maple syrup together in a small bowl and set aside.

3. Heat the oil in a large cast-iron skillet or wok over medium-high heat. When it shimmers, add the tofu in a single layer; it will sizzle on contact. Cook undisturbed until deeply browned, 4 to 5 minutes. Turn and brown the second side.

4. Remove the tofu from the pan and set aside on a large plate.

5. Add the cherry tomatoes and red onion to the same pan and let cook, stirring occasionally, until the tomatoes are blistered, 3 to 4 minutes. Smash about half of them gently with a wooden spoon.

6. Add the sambal–soy sauce mixture and cook briefly for a minute until thickened. Add the water and stir to combine. Add the tofu back to the pan. Bring to a simmer, then reduce the heat to the lowest setting, cover, and cook for 5 minutes.

7. Remove the lid and cook for another 5 to 10 minutes, until the sauce has thickened enough to coat the tofu.

8. Stir in the kosher salt and pepper to taste. Finish with a sprinkle of flaky salt and serve.

1 package (14 ounces/396 g) firm tofu

1 tablespoon cornstarch

2 tablespoons sambal oelek

1 teaspoon light soy sauce

1 teaspoon maple syrup

3 tablespoons neutral oil, such as canola or grapeseed

12 ounces (340 g) cherry or grape tomatoes, halved (2 cups)

½ red onion, sliced (about 3 ounces/100 g)

½ cup (120 g) water

¾ teaspoon kosher salt

Freshly ground black pepper

Flaky salt

**SUBSTITUTE:** If you don't have sambal oelek, sriracha can work (though it is more garlicky).

# FIVE-SPICE BRAISED SHORT RIBS WITH RICE CAKES

Serves 4

**Was there ever a cut more suitable for braising than short ribs? They're hard to mess up, and these are truly spectacular. I start by blanching them, as is traditional, to rid them of scum and excess blood. This step gives a clean braising liquid, which is scented with cumin, fennel, five-spice powder, and garlic. You can serve the short ribs whole with the rice cakes or shred the meat and toss it with the sauce.**

½ cup (120 g) Shaoxing wine, divided

1 scallion, trimmed

Two ⅛-inch-thick slices ginger

3 pounds (1365 g) bone-in beef short ribs

2 tablespoons five-spice powder, divided

2 tablespoons neutral oil

1 pound (455 g) Yukon gold potatoes, halved lengthwise

1 tablespoon cumin seeds

1 tablespoon fennel seeds

1 star anise

1 large yellow onion, roughly chopped (about 2 cups/330 g)

6 garlic cloves, peeled and smashed

3 cups (720 g) unsalted chicken stock

2 tablespoons light soy sauce

2 tablespoons brown sugar

2 strips lemon peel (avoid the white pith)

1 pound (455 g) fresh rice cakes (about 3 cups)

Kosher salt and freshly ground black pepper

Lemon wedges

1. Bring a large pot of salted water to a boil. Add 2 tablespoons of the Shaoxing wine and the scallion and ginger. Add the short ribs.

2. Return water to a boil, remove the short ribs and discard the liquid. Let the short ribs cool slightly. Pat dry with paper towels and sprinkle all sides with 1 tablespoon of the five-spice powder.

3. Heat the oil over medium-high heat in a heavy-bottomed pot, such as a Dutch oven, large enough to fit the short ribs in a single layer. Sear the short ribs until browned on all sides, about 10 minutes total. Transfer them to a plate. Drain all but 2 tablespoons of the fat.

4. Place the potatoes cut side down in the hot fat and let cook over medium heat, undisturbed, until golden brown, 5 to 6 minutes. Transfer the potatoes to a bowl.

5. If there is no fat left in the pot, add a splash of oil. When it's hot, add the remaining 1 tablespoon five-spice powder, the cumin seeds, fennel seeds, and star anise, and sauté until fragrant, about 30 seconds. Add the onion and garlic and sauté until translucent, 5 to 8 minutes.

6. Add the remaining Shaoxing wine, the stock, light soy sauce, dark soy sauce, brown sugar, and lemon peel, scraping up any browned bits from the bottom of the pot. Bring to a simmer, then gently submerge the short ribs into the sauce in a single layer. Add the potatoes, snuggling them between the short ribs. (The liquid should come half to three-quarters of the way up the short ribs.) Turn the heat to low, cover, and cook until fork-tender, about 2½ hours.

7. Remove the lid and simmer over medium-high for another 25 to 30 minutes, until the liquid has reduced to a gravy-like thickness.

8. Gently remove the short ribs and potatoes and cover to keep warm. Use a large spoon to carefully skim off the fat that has risen to the surface.

9. Add the rice cakes and cook, stirring occasionally to keep them from sticking, until they're chewy and soft, 8 to 10 minutes. Season with salt and pepper.

10. Divide the rice cakes, short ribs, and potatoes between four plates, spooning the gravy over them. Serve with lemon wedges for squeezing.

# BRAISED CABBAGE AND CHORIZO

Serves 4

**Cabbage is the queen of pantry vegetables. It's sturdy, durable, and lasts for a good while in the fridge. Cutting it into wedges and charring it caramelizes the edges, giving it a smoky sweetness. The cabbage is steam-braised in a chorizo gravy on low heat so it takes on the warm, hearty flavors of the gravy.**

1. Heat the oil in a large, deep heavy-bottomed skillet or Dutch oven over medium-high heat until it shimmers.

2. Place the cabbage wedges in the pan in a single layer and sear undisturbed for 6 to 8 minutes.

3. Sprinkle the exposed side of the cabbage with a pinch of salt. Turn and sear that side, another 5 to 6 minutes. Carefully remove the cabbage and set aside on a plate.

4. Fry the chorizo in the same pan, stirring often until the sausage is browned all over and has rendered its fat, 4 to 6 minutes. Use a slotted spoon to transfer the sausage to a small bowl.

5. If the pan seems dry, add a splash of oil. Add the scallions, garlic, dried chiles (if using), and ginger and fry until aromatic, about 1 minute.

6. Add the flour and whisk until a smooth, slightly darkened roux forms, 3 to 4 minutes.

7. Gradually add the stock, ¼ cup (60 g) at a time, to deglaze the pot, whisking and scraping up any browned bits after each addition. Sprinkle with the remaining salt and ¼ teaspoon black pepper.

8. Return the cabbage wedges and chorizo to the pan, nestling them into the gravy. Reduce the heat to low, cover, and braise until almost tender, about 15 minutes.

9. Remove the lid and simmer gently for another 10 minutes, stirring occasionally, until the cabbage is completely tender and the gravy is thick and emulsified.

10. Season with more salt and pepper, drizzle with the balsamic vinegar, and serve.

2 tablespoons neutral oil

1 small head green cabbage (about 2 pounds/910 g), quartered

1 teaspoon kosher salt, divided, plus more as needed

6 ounces (170 g) fresh Mexican chorizo sausage, sliced ¼ inch thick

4 scallions, trimmed and thinly sliced

4 garlic cloves, thinly sliced

2 dried red Sichuan chile peppers, stemmed and roughly chopped (optional, if more heat is desired)

One ¼-inch-thick slice ginger

2 teaspoons all-purpose flour

1½ cups (360 g) unsalted chicken stock or whatever stock you have

¼ teaspoon freshly ground black pepper, plus more as needed

2 teaspoons balsamic vinegar

**NOTE:** If you're using a very spicy brand of chorizo, you might want to omit the dried chile peppers.

# SOY-BRAISED MUSHROOMS WITH JAPANESE CURRY

Serves 4

**Mushrooms are quick to braise and release their umami-packed juices into the liquid. For this dish, choose sturdy mushrooms such as trumpets, cremini, or shiitakes. I keep the caps intact so they hold their shape in the braise. The mushrooms are first braised in a soy sauce braising liquid, which is later seasoned with a cube of kare (Japanese curry roux). They retain a sweet-savory flavor from the braise, but swim in a thickened curry-like sauce, a perfect combination of flavors.**

2 tablespoons neutral oil, such as canola or grapeseed

1 pound (455 g) mixed mushrooms (I like a mix of cremini, shiitake, and trumpets), stems trimmed

4 garlic cloves, minced

2 cups (480 g) unsalted chicken stock, whatever stock you have, or water

2 tablespoons Shaoxing wine

1 tablespoon light soy sauce

1 tablespoon brown sugar

1 teaspoon dark soy sauce

¼ teaspoon ground white pepper

12 ounces (340 g) baby potatoes (any color), halved (3 cups)

6 ounces (170 g) cipollini onions, peeled and halved (about 1½ cups)

1 cube (1 ounce/30 g) Japanese curry roux, such as S&B Golden Curry, or 2 tablespoons Japanese curry powder such as S&B

2 scallions, trimmed and thinly sliced

Cooked white rice

1. Heat a heavy-bottomed pot, such as a Dutch oven, over medium heat. Add the oil. When it shimmers, add the mushrooms and brown undisturbed until they just begin to release their juices, approximately 5 minutes.

2. Add the garlic and stir-fry until fragrant, approximately 1 minute.

3. Stir in the stock or water, Shaoxing wine, light soy sauce, brown sugar, dark soy sauce and white pepper. Bring to a boil over high heat, then reduce the heat to keep the liquid at a gentle simmer.

4. Add the potatoes and cipollini onions. Cover the pot partially and braise on low for 20 to 30 minutes, until the liquid has reduced so it comes half to three-quarters of the way up the sides of the mushrooms.

5. Add the curry roux cube or curry powder and stir to dissolve. Simmer uncovered, stirring occasionally, for another 10 minutes or until thickened.

6. Sprinkle with the scallions and serve with the rice.

**NOTE:** I like S&B Japanese curry, but any brand will work. Not all commercial curry roux are vegetarian, so if this is important to you, check the ingredient list on the package. If you want to omit the kare cube, I promise the soy sauce braising liquid is good on its own as well.

**SUBSTITUTE:** If you're using dried shiitakes, pour 2 to 3 cups hot water over approximately 3 ounces (85 g) and soak them for 15 minutes or until soft. Cut off the stems.

# BUTTERY CORN-BRAISED TOFU

Serves 4

**Home-style tofu—soy sauce–braised soft tofu loaded with vegetables and mushrooms, spooned over rice—is one of my favorite meals. The hallmark of the dish is its contrasting textures. Soft or silken tofu is fried to crisp its outside, while the inside remains pudding-like. This recipe starts from the same idea, giving the tofu a quick deep-fry to seal in its custardy texture. Then it takes off in a different direction, with the tofu braising in a luxuriously smooth strained corn puree. The theme of textural contrast is continued by topping the tofu and corn braising bath with fried caramelized whole corn kernels and fried and fresh scallions.**

1. Cut the tofu into 8 squares, about ½ inch thick. Transfer them to a paper towel–lined plate. Let sit for 30 minutes at room temperature to drain any residual liquid.

2. Heat about 1 inch of neutral oil in a wok or deep pot (preferably using a splash guard) to 375°F. Fry the tofu in two batches until it has a golden crust, about 3 minutes. Set aside on a paper towel–lined plate to drain.

3. Place 2 cups of the corn and 1 cup water in a blender and blend until very smooth. Strain through a fine-mesh sieve and discard the skins left behind. You should have 2 cups corn puree.

4. Heat the butter in a wok or Dutch oven over medium-low heat until foaming. Add the garlic and ginger and fry until fragrant, about 1 minute.

5. Add the corn puree, remaining ½ cup water, 1 tablespoon of the soy sauce, the Shaoxing wine, white pepper, salt, sugar, and cayenne pepper and stir to combine. Bring to a simmer, then reduce the heat to low. Stir in the cornstarch slurry.

6. Gently add the fried tofu—it is delicate, despite the crust. Spoon the braising liquid gently over it, partially cover, and simmer for 10 minutes.

7. Remove the lid and cook for another 5 minutes. The braising liquid will have thickened, coating the tofu.

8. While the tofu braises, heat the olive oil in a large skillet over medium heat. Add the remaining 1 cup corn kernels. Let cook and brown, stirring occasionally, for 2 to 3 minutes. When the corn kernels begin to pop in the pan, they are ready. Add half of the scallions and cook until fragrant.

9. Remove from the heat and stir in the remaining 1 teaspoon soy sauce, allowing it to erupt in a flurry of bubbling; it will caramelize in the process. Stir in the remaining scallions.

10. Put the tofu and its braising liquid in a shallow serving bowl, then sprinkle the caramelized corn-scallion mixture on top. Season with flaky salt and black pepper and serve.

1 block (1 pound/455 g) soft tofu

Neutral oil, such as canola or grapeseed

3 cups (750 g) corn kernels, divided

1½ cups (360 g) water, divided

2 tablespoons unsalted butter

3 garlic cloves, minced

1 teaspoon minced peeled ginger

1 tablespoon plus 1 teaspoon light soy sauce, divided

2 teaspoons Shaoxing wine

½ teaspoon ground white pepper

½ teaspoon kosher salt

½ teaspoon sugar

¼ teaspoon cayenne pepper

1 teaspoon cornstarch mixed with 1 tablespoon water

1 tablespoon extra-virgin olive oil

2 scallions, trimmed and thinly sliced, divided

Flaky salt and freshly ground black pepper

# GARLIC-BRAISED QUAIL EGGS

Serves 4

Whenever I have hot pot, I like to add canned quail eggs and let them steep-braise in the flavorful liquid. These eggs were inspired by that idea. They are simmered with a lot of garlic and a touch of soy sauce, and the flavors are warmed with black peppercorns and cardamom. After the initial braise, the eggs are steeped in a spiced mixture overnight so the flavors permeate them. The yolks stay soft and tender, unlike the yolks of chicken eggs. The braising liquid also intensifies as it sits, making it a great broth for spooning over rice.

2 tablespoons neutral cooking oil, such as grapeseed or canola

2 heads garlic, cloves separated and peeled (about 20 cloves)

5 green cardamom pods, crushed

1 teaspoon cracked black peppercorns

1 tablespoon red wine vinegar

1 tablespoon soy sauce

1 tablespoon honey

1 teaspoon kosher salt

2 or 3 strips dried mandarin orange peel

2 cups (480 g) unsalted chicken stock or whatever stock you have

20 cooked, peeled quail eggs (from a 15-ounce/425 g can)

Juice of 1 lemon

2 scallions, trimmed and finely chopped

1. Heat the oil in a large heavy pot, such as a Dutch oven, over medium-low heat. Add the garlic and cook until the edges are tinged with golden brown, 2 to 3 minutes.

2. Add the cardamom pods and peppercorns and fry for 1 minute.

3. Stir in the red wine vinegar, soy sauce, honey, and salt and cook until small bubbles form, then add the orange peel and stock. Add the quail eggs. Turn the heat up to bring to a simmer, then reduce the heat to low, cover, and cook for 20 minutes or until the quail eggs have started to take on some color from the braise.

4. Remove from the heat and let cool.

5. Refrigerate, still covered, and let steep for at least 4 hours or overnight.

6. Just before serving, gently warm the eggs on the stove over low heat. Serve warm.

**NOTE:** You can either hard-boil fresh quail eggs yourself or better yet, use canned cooked and peeled quail eggs in water. I prefer canned for ease and efficiency, since peeling so many small eggs can be time consuming. The canned eggs are found in Asian grocery stores or online.

**SUBSTITUTE:** You can use 8 chicken eggs; the timing will be similar.

# 熘/拌

*liū / bàn*

# SAUCE

This will probably come as no surprise to you, but much of Chinese cooking, like Western cooking, doesn't involve just one technique. It's more a Venn diagram of overlapping techniques, with steaming sometimes included in stir-frying, or boiling taking place before braising. Saucing, too, requires other cooking methods. This chapter focuses on sauce as the main driver behind flavor.

While saucing is a familiar concept across many cuisines, Chinese cooking recognizes two general methods for applying that sauce.

## FRY AND COAT IN STICKY SAUCE 熘 *liū*

The sauce is usually applied just off the heat, and it relies on the residual heat of the just-cooked food to meld the flavors. This method comes from northeastern China and has been popularized through take-out dishes like orange chicken. The chicken is deep-fried to create a crispy crunch, then tossed in the sauce. I treat mushrooms the same way in this chapter. *Liū* is distinct from a saucy stir-fry, where the quickly mixed sauce is an integral part of the cooking process and depends on the stove's heat and circulating movement.

Saucing doesn't necessarily mean deep-frying for the initial step. The food can be deep-fried or lightly fried. I don't often deep- fry in my home kitchen, but I do a lot of pan-frying. A deep-fry is employed if you are aiming for a crispy, crunchy exterior to soak up the sauce. The style of frying can also depend on the type of food being cooked: while mushrooms need deep-frying to develop a crispy coating, Brussels sprouts can get a crusty exterior from just a light dusting of cornstarch and a deep roasting, while tofu can be pan-fried.

## MIX AND COAT IN SAUCE 拌 *bàn*

Here the sauce is treated like a dressing and mixed in. Classic examples of 拌 *bàn* include cold sesame noodles, dried noodles with sauce, or salads. The cooked food is tossed with a premade sauce, usually off the heat. This method is all about concentrating flavor in the sauce. For that reason, strongly flavored ingredients like chile crisp, confits, strongly flavored vinegars, or pickled ingredients like capers and olives are often used.

Sauced noodles, 拌面, *bàn miàn*, aka saucy noodles, or dried sauced noodles, is one of my favorite ways to eat noodles. The sauce can be prepared any way, with many riffable possibilities: mixed, then tossed with noodles, like a vinaigrette; heated, then added to noodles; or stir-fried so it can cling to the noodles. Nor does the sauce have to be complicated—it can be as simple as pouring sizzling oil over aromatics or a soy and black vinegar–based sauce (see **Yóu Pō Miàn, page 166,** for a great example). The toppings, too, are endless: scallions, freshly minced ginger, crispy soybeans, crisped garlic or shallots, oils, condiments like sriracha sauce, mung bean sprouts, herbs, and more.

Whether you use liū or bàn, the 汁 *zhī* (sauce) is crucial. It can be made up of condiments and used as is, without any other step, or it can be simmered on the stovetop, with heat as an adjunct. It usually has a mix of fat (sesame oil, butter), sweet (sugar, honey, maple syrup), sour (a vinegar such as black vinegar or balsamic vinegar, or citrus or pickles), salt (soy sauce, salt, miso, oyster sauce), aromatics (minced garlic and other spices), and sometimes heat (chile oil, peppercorns, gochujang, harissa, sambal). The thickness of the gravy can come either from a reduction on the stove, from a condiment such as sesame paste, or by introducing a slurry of cornstarch and water.

In making sauces, as we've seen in other recipes in this book, there's no need to stick to traditional limits. In our contemporary kitchens, with pantries stocked with what's available—and these days, a wide variety of ingredients *are* more easily accessible—we can reach for whatever we want to create a balanced sauce and put it over almost

# HOT AND SOUR COLD NOODLES

酸辣鸡丝凉面 | *suān là jī sī liáng miàn* | Serves 2

**This traditional noodle dish is a popular street food in Sichuan, particularly in the summer. The chicken is cooked quite simply, shredded, then seasoned. The sauce is simmered and used to flavor both the cold noodles and the chicken. The seasoned shredded chicken adds a layer of texture and a complementary flavor to the bold sauce.**

1. **Poach the chicken breast**: Bring a medium saucepan with enough water to submerge the chicken to a boil. Add the scallion, ginger, star anise, and whole Sichuan peppercorns and simmer for 3 minutes.

2. Add the chicken and bring the water back to a boil. Immediately turn the heat to low and simmer for 5 minutes. Remove from the heat and cover tightly. Let sit for 10 minutes while you prepare an ice water bath.

3. Remove the chicken from the poaching liquid and place it in the ice water bath. (Discard the poaching liquid and spices.) Once the chicken has cooled, tear it into shreds by hand or with a fork. Combine the chicken in a medium bowl with the chile crisp, black vinegar, soy sauce, crushed Sichuan peppercorns, and sugar. Let sit for 15 minutes.

4. **Make the sauce:** Combine the garlic, sugar, white pepper, ¼ cup (60 g) water, soy sauce, and 2 tablespoons of the black vinegar in a small saucepan. Bring to a boil, then reduce the heat and simmer for about 5 minutes, until there are small bubbles and the sauce has thickened. Remove from the heat and let cool. Stir in the chile crisp, sesame oil, and the remaining 1 teaspoon black vinegar. Stir in the sesame paste.

5. **Cook the noodles and assemble**: Bring a large saucepan of water to a boil. Add the noodles, stir, and cook until al dente. Drain the noodles and rinse with cold water.

6. Divide the noodles between two bowls and top with the shredded chicken, cucumber, finely chopped scallions, and peanuts. Divide the sauce between the two bowls, mix, and serve.

**NOTE:** For the wheat noodles, you want a variety that's long, chewy, and bouncy, such as fresh Lanzhou ramen noodles or longevity noodles, or Shan Dong dried noodles.

**SUBSTITUTE:** A quickly fried tofu, such as **Harissa-Glazed Torn Tofu (page 176)** works nicely here instead of the chicken.

3 scallions, 1 cut into 3 sections and 2 finely chopped

One ¼-inch-thick slice ginger

1 piece star anise

1 teaspoon whole red Sichuan peppercorns

One 6-ounce (170 g) boneless, skinless chicken breast

1 tablespoon **Fried Shallot Chile Crisp (page 207)**

1 tablespoon black vinegar

1 teaspoon light soy sauce

½ teaspoon crushed red Sichuan peppercorns

½ teaspoon sugar

8 ounces (225 g) fresh thin wheat noodles

¼ cup julienned cucumber

2 tablespoons crushed salted, roasted peanuts

## HOT AND SOUR SAUCE

3 garlic cloves, minced

1 tablespoon sugar

½ teaspoon ground white pepper

2 tablespoons light soy sauce

2 tablespoons plus 1 teaspoon black vinegar, divided

1 tablespoon **Fried Shallot Chile Crisp (page 207)**

1 teaspoon toasted sesame oil

1 tablespoon sesame paste

# OIL-SIZZLED HAND-PULLED NOODLES

油泼面 | *Yóu Pō Miàn* | Serves 4

These noodles, sometimes called "biang biang" noodles, are named for the noise made during the shaping and pulling process—when the strip of noodle slaps the work surface, making a "biang" noise. The technique helps create a chewy texture. The noodles are divided among individual serving bowls. A premixed, unheated sauce is poured into each bowl, then an aromatic seasoning mix is piled on top. These separate components are brought together with a dramatic pour of hot oil, which not only blooms the aromatics but also heats up the sauce. You could mix it into the noodles before serving, but better yet, let each person toss their noodles at the table, so they can experience the sauce coming together.

## NOODLE DOUGH

2½ cups minus 1 tablespoon (300 g) all-purpose flour, plus more for dusting

½ teaspoon kosher salt

¾ cup (175 g) warm water, plus more as needed

Neutral oil, such as canola or grapeseed

## AROMATIC MIX

5 garlic cloves, minced

2 scallions, trimmed and thinly sliced

1 teaspoon crushed red or green Sichuan peppercorns

1 teaspoon red pepper flakes

½ teaspoon ground white pepper

½ teaspoon kosher salt

¼ teaspoon sugar

*Ingredients Continue*

1. **Make the noodle dough**: You can make the dough in a stand mixer or by hand.

   **STAND MIXER METHOD:** Fit a stand mixer with the dough hook and mix the flour and salt. Gently stream in the warm water on low speed. Keep mixing until a dough forms. Turn the speed to medium-low and mix until the sides of the bowl and the surface of the dough are clean and smooth but the dough is still tacky to the touch, about 12 minutes. If the dough is too dry, add a little water, 1 tablespoon at a time, and mix to incorporate it.

   **HAND METHOD:** Combine the flour and salt in a large bowl. Gently stream in the water while stirring with chopsticks in your other hand. Mix until a loose dough forms. Knead for 12 to 15 minutes, until the dough, your hands, and the sides of the bowl are clean and smooth.

2. Cover and rest the dough for 5 minutes. Transfer the dough to a lightly floured surface and knead for another 5 minutes. (This may take a bit of strength.) Regardless of how you mixed it, the ball of dough should be tacky but well formed, elastic, and smooth. If you break off a piece of it, you should be able to stretch it a few inches without breaking. If it is not there yet, give it a 5-minute rest and 5-minute knead. Cover with plastic wrap and let rest at room temperature for 1½ hours.

3. Divide the dough into four portions. (Each portion will be an individual serving.) On a floured surface and using a floured rolling pin or your palms, flatten each portion of dough into a small rectangle, about 2 by 6 inches. Brush the rectangles with oil, stack them on top of each other, then wrap in plastic wrap and refrigerate overnight or for up to 3 days. Bring to room temperature before continuing. Or you can let the dough rest for 1 hour at room temperature.

4. **Make the aromatic mix:** Stir the garlic, scallions, Sichuan peppercorns, red pepper flakes, white pepper, salt, and sugar in a small bowl.

5. **Make the sauce:** Stir together the light soy sauce, water, black vinegar, dark soy sauce, and sugar in another small bowl.

6. Bring a large pot of water to a boil, because the noodles shouldn't sit at room temperature for long.

7. **Pull the noodles:** Work with one dough rectangle at a time on an oiled surface, keeping the remaining portions wrapped loosely in plastic. Use a chopstick to make an indentation in the center of a rectangle down its length, marking two long rectangles. Grasp the short ends of the rectangle, then start pulling gently. It should stretch easily. Once it is about 2 feet long, gently bounce the middle up and down against the countertop ("biang"), until the strand is about 4 feet long. It will form a gentle curve with your hands holding the ends, with the bottom of the curve hitting the work surface.

8. Using the indentation you created before, separate by ripping the dough through the indent with your hands into two 4-feet-long strands. Cover and repeat with the remaining pieces of dough.

9. Add all the noodles to the boiling water and stir to prevent sticking. Boil for about 2 minutes—the noodles should be chewy but not mushy.

10. Drain the noodles and divide among four bowls.

11. Divide the aromatic mix and then the sauce among the bowls, on top of the noodles.

12. **Sizzle the oil:** In a small saucepan (ideally with a spout for pouring), heat the oil over high heat until it shimmers. To test, place a wooden chopstick in the oil; the oil should bubble around it immediately.

13. Carefully pour the oil over the aromatics in a steady stream so that every bit gets bloomed.

14. Toss to coat the noodles, or let people do that at the table. Serve immediately.

### SAUCE

¼ cup light soy sauce

¼ cup water

3 tablespoons black vinegar

1 teaspoon dark soy sauce

2 tablespoons sugar

3 tablespoons neutral cooking oil

**NOTE:** If you don't have time to make noodles from scratch, you can substitute any store-bought wide noodles, such as knife-cut noodles or even pappardelle in a pinch.

# SWEET AND SOUR MUSHROOMS

Serves 4

**Traditional sweet and sour sauce is made with hawthorn fruit, which is little known in the US. Red and round, with a uniquely sweet, floral, slightly acidic flavor, it's often dried into chips or cooked into a jam in China. I used to bring a small pack of dried hawthorn berries with me to combat motion sickness on trips. Since they're not very common here, cooks have turned to ketchup as a substitute, but I prefer to use a fruit jam, which has brighter, fruity notes. In this recipe, mushrooms undergo a deep-fry to create a crispy exterior that the sauce can cling to.**

1. **Prepare the mushrooms:** Tear any larger mushrooms, such as maitake and king oyster, into 2-inch pieces. (You want to keep everything about the same size so that the mushrooms cook evenly during the frying process.)

2. Thoroughly whisk together the egg whites, salt, white pepper, and Shaoxing wine. In a separate shallow bowl, combine the rice flour with the starch.

3. **Make the sauce:** In a third small bowl, whisk together the water, Shaoxing wine, jam, rice vinegar, cornstarch, and chile peppers. Set aside.

4. Heat enough oil for frying, approximately 3 cups, in a large, deep pot or a wok over medium heat until the temperature reaches 350°F. To test, place a wooden chopstick in the oil; the oil should bubble around it immediately.

5. Working in batches, dip the mushrooms first in the egg white mixture, then dust evenly with the flour mixture. Fry the mushrooms, stirring to separate them, until they are golden brown, 5 to 6 minutes. Remove with a slotted spoon and transfer to a paper towel–lined baking sheet to drain. Repeat until you have fried all the mushrooms. Let the oil cool, then carefully pour it into a heatproof container for discarding or strain and store to reuse for another deep-fry.

6. Heat the oil in a separate large skillet over medium-high heat.

7. Add the garlic and sauté until fragrant. Add the scallions and jalapeños and stir-fry for another minute, until tender and aromatic.

8. Add the sauce and cook, stirring, until thickened, 2 to 3 minutes. Stir in the salt.

9. Remove the pan from the heat. Taste the sauce—it should be fruity and tangy. Add more vinegar, if desired, reducing the sauce again if necessary, and add more salt to taste. Add the fried mushrooms and toss to combine, until the sauce has thickened further and coats them. Serve with white rice.

## MUSHROOMS

10 ounces (300 g) mixed mushrooms, such as oyster, maitake, and/or king oyster

2 egg whites, at room temperature

1 teaspoon kosher salt

½ teaspoon ground white pepper

¼ cup Shaoxing wine

1 cup (120 g) water-milled glutinous rice flour

½ cup (76 g) sweet potato starch or potato starch

## SWEET AND SOUR SAUCE

½ cup water

2 tablespoons Shaoxing wine

3 tablespoons seedless red raspberry jam or other jam

2 tablespoons rice vinegar

2 teaspoons cornstarch

2 red Thai chile peppers, halved

2 garlic cloves, minced

2 scallions, trimmed and chopped

2 jalapeños roughly chopped

¼ teaspoon kosher salt, plus more to taste

About 3 cups plus 1 tablespoon neutral oil

# SPICY HONEYED BRUSSELS SPROUTS

Serves 4

**Creating a sauce can be an exploration of your favorite flavor profiles. Do you like something that tends to be more spicy, or tangy, or sticky? Practice balancing flavors. Something salty needs sweet as a balance, and spice often pairs well with tang. Whenever you add an ingredient to a sauce, think about what flavor it contributes, what texture or form it takes—liquid? solid? does it need to be dissolved?—and how heat can affect it.**

**This recipe highlights my favorite way to cook Brussels sprouts, roasting, which makes the leaves caramelized, nutty flavored, and crispy. Spicy sambal oelek unites with smoky paprika and honey to create a tangy, spicy, sweet, sticky sauce. The hot little sprouts are immediately tossed with the sauce, and the residual heat melds it to them.**

2 pounds (910 g) Brussels sprouts, trimmed and halved, or quartered if large

6 garlic cloves, peeled and lightly smashed

2 tablespoons extra-virgin olive oil or other cooking oil

2 tablespoons cornstarch

½ teaspoon kosher salt

¼ teaspoon freshly ground black pepper

## SAUCE

¼ cup (60 g) water

3 tablespoons honey

2 tablespoons sambal oelek

1 tablespoon rice vinegar

2 teaspoons dark soy sauce

1 teaspoon smoked paprika

½ teaspoon ground black pepper, plus more for serving

Lemon wedges

Flaky salt

1. Heat the oven to 425°F.
2. Toss the Brussels sprouts and garlic with the olive oil in a bowl, then lightly dust with the cornstarch, the salt, and black pepper. Spread on a baking sheet. Bake for 20 minutes or until the sprouts are crispy and their cut edges are browned.
3. **Meanwhile, make the sauce:** Whisk together the water, honey, sambal, rice vinegar, dark soy sauce, paprika, and black pepper in a small saucepan. Bring the sauce to a boil over medium-high heat, then reduce to low and simmer until it reaches the consistency of a barbecue sauce (thick and coating the back of a spoon), 10 to 15 minutes.
4. As soon as you remove the Brussels sprouts from the oven, pour the sauce over them on the baking sheet. Stir or toss to coat.
5. Serve with a squeeze of lemon and a sprinkle of flaky salt and black pepper.

# SWEET AND SPICY DELICATA SQUASH WITH BURRATA

Serves 2 to 4

**Delicata squash is ideal for this dish—it can be sliced thin, and it's delicate enough to be cooked on the stovetop. Its innate sweetness pairs well with a zingy sauce. After the squash slices are seared and pan-fried, they are coated with the sauce in the pan, with the heat bringing all the flavors together. Burrata cheese adds creaminess and balance.**

1. **Make the sauce:** Combine the water, balsamic vinegar, maple syrup, soy sauce, gochujang, dried chile peppers, ginger, and gochugaru in a small saucepan. Bring to a boil over high heat, then reduce the heat to low and simmer, stirring often, until the sauce is slightly thickened, with small, even bubbles on the surface, 5 to 7 minutes. Set aside.

2. Heat the neutral oil in a large skillet over medium heat until it shimmers. Add the squash in a single layer, working in batches if necessary, and let the slices brown undisturbed for 5 minutes. Turn and cook the other side for 3 to 4 minutes, until the squash is completely tender and easily pierced with a fork. Transfer to a plate while you cook the remainder of the squash.

3. Remove the pan from the heat. Return all the squash to the pan and immediately pour in the sauce. Toss the squash so that all the sides are coated. The sauce will bubble and thicken when it hits the hot pan, becoming glazy. (You can leave the ginger and chiles in.)

4. Transfer to a serving bowl and top with the scallions, sesame seeds, and burrata. Drizzle with sesame oil, sprinkle with flaky salt and pepper, and serve.

½ cup (120 g) water

2 tablespoons balsamic vinegar

2 tablespoons maple syrup

1 teaspoon light soy sauce

1 teaspoon gochujang

2 dried red Sichuan chile peppers, stemmed and smashed

One ¼-inch-thick slice ginger

1 teaspoon gochugaru

2 tablespoons neutral oil, such as canola or grapeseed

1½ pounds (680 g) delicata squash (1 large or 2 on the smaller side), halved lengthwise, seeds removed, and cut into ½-inch-thick slices

Thinly sliced scallions

Toasted sesame seeds

1 ball (4 ounces/115 g) burrata, at room temperature, or 2 balls if serving 4

Toasted sesame oil

Flaky salt and freshly ground black pepper

**NOTE:** Keep in mind that the spicy sauce will dominate, so be sure to adjust the seasonings to your preference.

**SUBSTITUTE:** You can use Honeynut squash or other delicate-fleshed squash in place of delicata.

# HARISSA-GLAZED TORN TOFU

Serves 4

**Pan-frying can give firm tofu a good crust for a sauce to cling to. This sauce is on the sweeter side, but it's nicely balanced by the hot chiles, scallions, earthy mushrooms, and a final squeeze of lemon juice. Feel free to taste-test it and adjust it to your preferences.**

**Tearing the tofu with your hands rather than cutting it with a knife gives it more craggy surfaces and texture, the better to hold the sauce.**

2 tablespoons honey

2 tablespoons water

1 tablespoon harissa

1 teaspoon rice vinegar

1 garlic clove, grated

1 pound (455 g) firm tofu, drained

2 tablespoons cornstarch

1 teaspoon ground white pepper

1 teaspoon kosher salt

3 tablespoons neutral cooking oil, such as canola or grapeseed, divided, plus more as necessary

6 ounces (170 g) mixed mushrooms, sliced or torn into ¼- to ½-inch pieces

2 red Thai chile peppers, stemmed and roughly chopped

2 scallions, trimmed and chopped into 1½-inch sections

Lemon wedges

Toasted sesame seeds

1. **Make the sauce:** Combine the honey, water, harissa, rice vinegar, and garlic in a small saucepan. Bring to a boil, reduce the heat to medium, and simmer until the sauce is thickened enough to lightly coat a spoon (it should be thinner than gravy), 1 to 2 minutes. Set aside.

2. Place the tofu block on a clean kitchen towel and squeeze to extract the liquid. (Since it's going to be torn anyway, you can be aggressive.) Tear the tofu into bite-sized pieces and place in a medium bowl. Sprinkle with the cornstarch, white pepper, and salt and toss to combine.

3. Heat a wok or nonstick skillet over medium-high heat. Pour in 2 tablespoons of the oil and heat until shimmering. Fry half the ripped tofu pieces until browned and crispy on all sides, 6 to 8 minutes. Transfer to a bowl. Add the remaining 1 tablespoon oil if the pan is dry and when it is hot, fry the remaining tofu. Add to the first batch.

4. Add the mushrooms to the pan and cook undisturbed over medium-high heat until golden brown, 4 to 5 minutes. Remove from the pan and set aside with the tofu.

5. If the pan is dry, add a small splash of oil. Add the chile peppers and scallions and stir-fry for about 30 seconds, until fragrant. Return the tofu and mushrooms to the pan, then add the sauce and toss to combine. Cook until the sauce has thickened and coats the tofu and mushrooms, 1 to 2 minutes.

6. Finish with a squeeze of lemon juice and a sprinkle of sesame seeds and serve.

**NOTE:** I don't usually weight the tofu to press out liquid, since by definition, firm tofu has already been drained and pressed. Instead, I just pour out the liquid from the box and lay the block on a paper towel to sponge up any drippings. However, for this dish, I do squeeze out the excess liquid, because the tofu needs to be as crispy as possible to hold the sauce.

# NOODLES WITH TOMATO-GARLIC CONFIT AND EGGS

Serves 2

**Along with fried rice, tomato-and-egg is the stir-fry often recommended as a gateway dish to learning how to cook Chinese. It's a much beloved, homey meal that seems to be a universally shared childhood memory among the children of Chinese immigrants. Here I play on that dish, ramping up the tomato flavor with tomato confit and tomato paste—a technique that's especially good when you have out-of-season fruit—to create a silky sauce that coats the fluffy curds of egg and the noodles.**

1. Bring a large pot of salted water to a boil. Add the noodles and cook according to the package instructions until al dente. Drain. Toss with the sesame oil to prevent them from sticking.

2. Put the confit, confit oil, water, and tomato paste in a blender and blitz until smooth. You should have about ⅔ cup. Set aside.

3. Whisk the eggs with the soy sauce in a bowl. Heat a well-seasoned wok or a nonstick skillet over medium-high heat. Add the neutral oil and swirl to coat. When the oil is shimmering, add the eggs and scramble to create large, fluffy curds. Set aside on a plate.

4. Add the cherry tomatoes to the same pan. Let them blister and start to express their juices, about 3 minutes.

5. Add the confit puree and mix to combine. Bring to a boil, then turn heat to low, and simmer for another 2 minutes, until thickened slightly. Season to taste, adding sugar if needed, depending on sweetness of the cherry tomatoes.

6. Add the scrambled eggs and toss to coat.

7. Divide the noodles between two bowls. Divide the tomato-egg mixture between the bowls. Mix to combine, top with the scallions, and serve.

8 ounces (225 g) fresh Chinese wheat noodles

1 teaspoon toasted sesame oil

¼ cup **Tomato-Garlic Confit (page 211)** plus 1 tablespoon of the confit oil

¼ cup water

1 tablespoon double-concentrate tomato paste

3 large eggs

1 teaspoon light soy sauce

2 tablespoons neutral oil, such as canola or grapeseed

6 ounces (170 g) cherry tomatoes (about 18)

1 teaspoon sugar (optional, depending on sweetness of your tomatoes)

2 scallions, trimmed and thinly sliced

**NOTE:** Double-concentrate tomato paste comes in a tube and is available in most supermarkets.

**SUBSTITUTE:** I use fresh Chinese wheat noodles, but you can use any noodle, such as bucatini, udon, or ramen.

# ZUCCHINI-SOBA NOODLE SALAD

Serves 4

**The sauce for these bàn miàn-style noodles gets a fruity, spicy lift from gochujang mellowed with tomato paste and honey. The gochujang is not meant to dominate—it is simply lending its sweet, fragrant flavors to the sauce. Capers and pickled red onion add tang and crunch. Often I throw in a handful of arugula for a lighter feel.**

Kosher salt

4 bundles soba noodles
(12.8 ounces/375 g total)

1 teaspoon toasted sesame oil

3 tablespoons black vinegar,
divided

2 tablespoons honey, divided

1 tablespoon neutral oil,
such as canola or grapeseed,
plus more as needed

2 large or 3 medium zucchini
(22 ounces/625 g total),
trimmed, sliced crosswise
¼ inch thick

¼ cup (60 g) water

1½ tablespoons tomato paste

1 tablespoon extra-virgin olive oil

2 teaspoons gochujang

1 garlic clove, grated

½ cup (75 g) **Quick-Pickled Red Onion with Peppercorns (page 230),** roughly chopped

2 tablespoons capers,
drained if in brine,
rinsed and drained if salted

Grated zest and juice of 1 lemon

2 handfuls of arugula (optional)

1. Bring a large pot of salted water to a boil. Add the soba noodles and cook, stirring occasionally to prevent sticking, until al dente, 3 to 4 minutes (check the directions on the package). Rinse thoroughly under cold water, drain well, and transfer to a large bowl. Drizzle with the sesame oil, toss to combine, and set aside.

2. Combine 1 tablespoon of the black vinegar with 1 tablespoon of the honey in a medium bowl and set aside.

3. Add the neutral oil to a large heavy-bottomed skillet over medium heat. Working in batches, add a single layer of zucchini slices and cook until golden and soft, 3 to 4 minutes per side. Remove with a slotted spoon and drain on a paper towel–lined plate, then quickly transfer to the bowl with the vinegar and honey mixture and toss to coat. Repeat with the remaining zucchini.

4. **Make the sauce:** Whisk together the water, the remaining 2 tablespoons black vinegar, tomato paste, olive oil, the remaining 1 tablespoon honey, the gochujang, and garlic. Pour over the noodles and toss to combine.

5. Add the red onion, capers, and lemon zest and juice. Add the zucchini slices along with any remaining marinade, and the arugula (if using), and toss to combine.

6. Serve immediately or let sit in the fridge and enjoy the flavors cold the next day.

# RIGATONI WITH SAUCY STIR-FRIED LAMB AND ASPARAGUS

Serves 2

**My friend Hetty McKinnon, author of *To Asia with Love* and *Tenderheart*, points out that a stir-fry can top not just rice, as it traditionally does, but any starch. Here, I make a bold, saucy stir-fry of asparagus and crispy ground lamb seasoned with warm spices that is quickly married to rigatoni in the wok.**

1. Bring a large pot of salted water to a boil. Add the rigatoni, stir to prevent sticking, and cook until al dente. Scoop out 1 cup of the pasta water and set aside. Drain the pasta and toss with the sesame oil to prevent sticking. Set aside.

2. Mix together the soy sauce, oyster sauce, black vinegar, and maple syrup in a small bowl.

3. Heat a wok or large skillet over medium-high heat until hot. Add the neutral oil and heat until it shimmers. Add the lamb. Use a spatula to press it against the pan for maximal contact so it gets crispy bits and the fat renders. Cook undisturbed until the lamb is crispy and browned, about 3 minutes. Use your spatula to break it up into bite-sized pieces and turn to brown on the other side, about 2 minutes.

4. Add the garlic, ginger, cumin, paprika, salt, and black pepper, tossing to combine. Add the asparagus and stir-fry until it is green and tender but retains a crunch, about 3 minutes.

5. Add the soy sauce mixture and the reserved pasta cooking water to the pan. Stir and simmer for 5 minutes or until reduced to about one third. Add the cornstarch slurry and continue to simmer until thickened, another 3 minutes.

6. When the sauce is thick enough to coat the back of a spoon, add the pasta and stir to combine. Season with salt and pepper.

7. Turn off the heat, and finish with a swirl of crème fraîche, a squeeze of lemon, and the scallions and serve.

Kosher salt

1 pound (455 g) rigatoni

1 teaspoon toasted sesame oil

1 tablespoon light soy sauce

1 tablespoon oyster sauce

1 tablespoon black vinegar

1 teaspoon maple syrup

1 tablespoon neutral oil

12 ounces (340 g) ground lamb

3 garlic cloves, minced

1 teaspoon minced peeled ginger

2 teaspoons ground cumin

1 teaspoon hot paprika

¼ teaspoon freshly ground black pepper, plus more as needed

8 ounces (225 g) asparagus, tough ends trimmed, sliced on an angle into 1-inch segments

1 teaspoon cornstarch mixed with 1 tablespoon water

1 tablespoon crème fraîche

Lemon wedge

2 scallions, trimmed and thinly sliced

**NOTE:** You can use any large, textured pasta that sauce will cling to, such as fusilli or cavatappi, instead of the rigatoni.

# CRISPY CHORIZO AND TOMATO OVER SILKEN TOFU

Serves 4

**Silken tofu is almost like a savory pudding and so makes a great recipe base. Traditional Chinese recipes involve topping a block of the silken tofu with a soy-based sauce and preserved thousand-year eggs, or just soy sauce and scallions. In Japan, hiyayakko (cold tofu) is garnished with shiso and served chilled, a refreshing dish for warm days. In this recipe, I heap crispy ground chorizo, bathed in a gravy made from caramelized tomato paste, over the chilled silken tofu. The dish features contrasting textures and flavors: crispy versus silky and spicy versus creamy.**

1 block (1 pound/455 g) silken tofu

1 tablespoon neutral oil, such as canola or grapeseed, plus more as necessary

6 ounces (170 g) ground Mexican chorizo

1 shallot, thinly sliced

2 garlic cloves, minced

1 tablespoon double-concentrate tomato paste

¼ cup (60 g) unsalted chicken stock or water

1 tablespoon light soy sauce

2 teaspoons light brown sugar

Kosher salt and freshly ground black pepper

2 scallions, trimmed and thinly sliced

Cooked white rice

1. Line a plate with paper towels, then gently invert the silken tofu block onto the towels and let drain for 5 minutes.

2. Meanwhile, heat the oil in a large skillet over medium-high heat. Add the ground chorizo and, using a spatula, flatten it in the pan. Let cook undisturbed until crispy, 2 to 3 minutes.

3. Use the spatula to turn the chorizo and crisp the other side, 2 to 3 minutes. Break it up into bite-sized, crispy pieces. With the spatula or a slotted spoon, transfer the chorizo to a small bowl and set aside.

4. There should be rendered fat in the pan, but if it's dry, add a splash of oil. Add the shallot and garlic, reduce the heat to medium, and sauté until softened and beginning to brown, 3 to 4 minutes.

5. Add the tomato paste and stir to coat the alliums. Cook, stirring frequently, until the paste has darkened and caramelized, about 5 minutes.

6. Stir in the stock or water, soy sauce, and brown sugar and mix to combine. Return the chorizo to the pan. Simmer for 2 to 3 minutes to meld the sauce and chorizo. Season with salt and black pepper to taste.

7. Place the tofu gently on a serving plate and top with the tomato-chorizo sauce. Sprinkle with the scallions. Spoon over rice to serve.

**SUBSTITUTE:** If you can't find ground chorizo, you can substitute ground pork. Just add ½ teaspoon smoked paprika and ½ teaspoon fennel seeds to the pork.

# YÓU PŌ ORZO WITH FRIED HALLOUMI

Serves 4

**If pasta salad and Yóu Pō Miàn were married, this dish would be their child. It features one of my favorite cheats with big results—the oil-sizzle method of creating a sauce—this time over orzo. It capitalizes on the quick bloom of aromatics and spices with a hot fat—here, butter and a hint of soy sauce. The buttery sauce coats the orzo, and the dish is balanced with a squeeze of fresh lemon and potent, briny cubes of fried halloumi.**

1. Bring a medium saucepan of water to a boil over high heat and season with salt. Prepare an ice water bath. Remove the rough base from the bok choy, then tear into separate leaves. Add the bok choy to the boiling water and blanch for 1 to 2 minutes, until bright green. Use a slotted spoon to immediately transfer it to the water bath, leaving the pot of water over the heat.

2. When the water returns to a boil, add the orzo and cook according to the package directions until al dente. Drain and set aside.

3. When the bok choy is cool, remove from the water bath, gently squeeze dry, roughly chop, and set aside.

4. Cut the halloumi block lengthwise into two ½-inch-thick slabs. Dab with a paper towel to remove any residual brine. Heat 1 tablespoon of the oil in a large nonstick skillet or well-seasoned cast-iron skillet over medium heat. Fry the halloumi until golden brown on both sides, 2 to 3 minutes per side. Transfer to a cutting board. When the cheese is cool enough to handle, cut into ½-inch cubes and set aside.

5. Toss together the orzo, bok choy, and green olives in a large bowl.

6. Put the garlic, paprika, a pinch of salt, red pepper flakes, black pepper, and sugar in a small pile on top of the orzo and vegetables. Don't stir them in.

7. Heat the butter and 1 tablespoon oil in a small saucepan (preferably with a pour spout) over medium-low heat until the butter has completely melted and the mixture is bubbling. Add the soy sauce and simmer for 30 seconds, then immediately pour over the pile of aromatics.

8. Top with the pecorino, then mix thoroughly to combine. Fold in the scallions, lemon zest and juice, and halloumi. Season with flaky salt and black pepper to taste and serve immediately.

Kosher salt

2 or 3 small heads bok choy (8 ounces/225 g total)

8 ounces (225 g) orzo (about 1 cup)

1 block (8 ounces/225 g) halloumi cheese

2 tablespoons neutral oil, divided

2 tablespoons roughly chopped pitted green olives (4 or 5 olives)

3 garlic cloves, minced

1 teaspoon smoked paprika

½ teaspoon red pepper flakes

½ teaspoon freshly ground black pepper

½ teaspoon sugar

2 tablespoons unsalted butter

1 teaspoon light soy sauce

2 tablespoons freshly, finely grated pecorino cheese

2 scallions, trimmed and thinly sliced

Grated zest and juice of 1 lemon

Flaky salt and freshly ground black pepper

# GREEN PEPPERCORN–MARINATED GREEN LENTILS AND MUSHROOMS

Serves 4

**Green lentils are particularly amenable to absorbing flavor without losing their textural integrity. Although the cooking techniques behind this dish include elements of boil, sauce, and infuse, it's really the marinade that drives this dish. Green peppercorns have a subtle mouth-numbing heat as well as the aroma of citrus, and pair well with a vinegar-based marinade. The salad can be served warm immediately, though the flavors get even better with time.**

Kosher salt

1½ cups (350 g) French green lentils

½ cup plus 2 tablespoons (150 g) extra-virgin olive oil, divided, plus more as needed

6 ounces (170 g) mixed mushrooms such as shiitake, oyster, and/or maitake, cut or torn into ¼-inch-thick slices

2 strips dried mandarin orange peel

1 tablespoon julienned peeled ginger

1½ teaspoons finely crushed green Sichuan peppercorns

½ teaspoon red pepper flakes

3 garlic cloves, grated

1 tablespoon cumin seeds

1 teaspoon fennel seeds

⅓ cup (80 g) rice vinegar

¼ cup (60 g) unsalted chicken or vegetable stock

1 tablespoon light soy sauce

1 teaspoon sugar

1 tablespoon grated orange zest (from 1 large navel orange)

Freshly ground black pepper

Crème fraîche

Cilantro leaves

1. Bring a medium saucepan of salted water to a boil over high heat. Add the lentils and bring back to a boil. Reduce the heat to medium and simmer uncovered for 15 to 20 minutes, until the lentils are cooked through but still firm enough to hold their shape. Drain and set aside.

2. Heat 2 tablespoons of the olive oil in a wok or large skillet over medium heat. Add the mushrooms and stir-fry until brown, 6 to 8 minutes. Set aside in a small bowl.

3. In same pan, combine the remaining ½ cup (120 g) olive oil, the mandarin orange peel, ginger, green peppercorns, and red pepper flakes. Simmer over medium-low heat for 3 to 4 minutes, until aromatic, stirring constantly and being careful not to burn anything. Remove from the heat. Add the garlic, cumin seeds, and fennel seeds and stir to combine.

4. Stir in the mushrooms, vinegar, stock, soy sauce, and sugar and mix to combine. Add the lentils and stir. Sprinkle with the orange zest and season with salt and black pepper to taste.

5. When you're ready to serve, transfer to a serving dish and top with a tablespoon of crème fraîche and some cilantro. Serve warm, room temperature, or cold.

**SUBSTITUTE:** You can use black beluga lentils instead of or in addition to the green lentils.

# OKRA WITH LEMON CRÈME FRAÎCHE AND FRIED GARLIC

Serves 4

**Okra can be polarizing because of its texture, specifically, the viscous texture that comes with the vegetable. I never quite appreciated it until I had a Sichuan-style dish with poached okra, garlic, and a vinegar-based chile crisp sauce. It turns out that chilling the okra smooths out its gummy texture a bit and makes it reminiscent of Japanese natto (fermented soybeans). I pair it with a tangy, creamy sauce and finish with crispy garlic for textural contrast.**

1. Bring a large pot of salted water to a boil and prepare an ice water bath. Blanch the okra for 2 minutes, then transfer with a slotted spoon to the water bath. The okra will be bright green.

2. When it's cold, drain the okra. Cut off the stem end from each one, then slice in half lengthwise. Set aside in a serving bowl.

3. **Make the sauce:** Slice the ends off the lemon. Standing it upright on a flat end, carefully slice off the skin, white pith, and membrane and discard. Finely chop the flesh and discard any seeds. Mix together the lemon flesh, crème fraîche, olive oil, scallion, ¼ teaspoon kosher salt, and ½ teaspoon pepper.

4. Heat the neutral oil in a wok over medium heat and swirl to coat. Add the garlic slices and cook, stirring constantly, until they are pale golden brown, 2 to 2½ minutes. Remove the pan from heat, then use a slotted spoon to transfer the garlic to a small bowl. Reserve the oil.

5. Pour the crème fraîche sauce over the okra, then add the garlic. Finish with a drizzle of the reserved garlic oil, a sprinkle of flaky salt, and a pinch of black pepper, and serve.

Kosher salt

10 ounces (300 g) okra

1 lemon

2 tablespoons crème fraîche

1 tablespoon extra-virgin olive oil

1 scallion, trimmed and finely minced

½ teaspoon freshly ground black pepper, plus more for serving

2 tablespoons neutral oil, such as canola or grapeseed

3 garlic cloves, sliced

Flaky salt

# áo

# INFUSE

Whereas most people know what a stir-fry is, the Chinese cooking technique of infusing is less familiar. If I say the words "chile oil," though, you'll immediately understand both the principle and its power. Infusing—the process of extracting (熬制 *áo zhì*) and transferring taste from one medium to another—is key to some of my favorite flavor-filled dishes, from scallion oil noodles to lip-smacking broths and herbal soups. Infusion is what makes a seemingly simple dish complex.

Herbs, aromatics, chiles, meat, or vegetables can all be infused into oils or liquids. Depending on the intensity and type of flavor desired, infusing can be quick, like sizzling oil poured over aromatics, or long and slow as in confits, where ingredients like leeks or tomato and garlic are cooked for hours in oil until they release their essence. Infusion is everywhere, but it's especially important in soups and flavored oils.

## SOUP 汤 *tāng*

Many Chinese soups are clear enough to "see the bottom of the pot," as my father-in-law says when describing 腌笃鲜 *yān dǔ xiān* (double pork soup), one of his favorite clear soups. Yet these soups are fragrant and full of flavor, thanks to infusion. Bones, herbs, aromatics, preserved foods such as dried scallops, shiitakes, and meats like salt pork are all tapped for their potential in stocks—a process called 熬汤 *áo tāng*, to brew soup. For example, 上汤 *shàng tāng*, the stock commonly used in Cantonese cuisine, draws on the flavors of chicken, pork, ham, and scallops, while 高汤 *gāo tāng* (high stock) is usually a combination of poultry, pork, and seafood. It's considered an ultimate stock because of the flavors drawn from three different types of meat, hence the name "high." There is also 清汤 *qīng tāng* (clear soup), which as the name implies specifically prizes

purity and clarity. These soups are less about the additions and more about having a rich stock to slurp, so the ingredients are usually cut smaller. They are often served by themselves, for example at breakfast in lieu of coffee, or alongside a meal. Soups, in general, are thought to be healing, so they are often served when someone is recovering from an illness or is in need of a boost.

## "OIL-SIZZLE" 油淋 *yóu lín*

Pouring sizzling oil over aromatics is a way of dressing raw, cooked, cold, or hot food with a burst of flavor extraction. The aromatics, such as scallions, garlic, and ginger, or spices like red pepper flakes, are scattered on top of the dish; the hot oil releases their flavors and becomes infused with them. The oil then becomes part of the finishing step, as in **Yóu Pō Miàn (page 166).** This technique is commonly used to present steamed fish, but it also works wonders with vegetables like celtuce.

## INFUSE INTO OIL 熬油 *áo yóu*

I could write love letters to this method. A classic example is Shanghainese scallion oil, in which the scallions are toasted low and slow in oil, then combined with soy sauce and tossed with noodles. The main flavor comes not from the soy, but from the scallion oil itself. I use the same principle to infuse other alliums into oil, such as garlic, shallots, and leeks. The duration of the infusion and the temperature of the oil dictate the flavor (a quick sizzle of scallions will impart a different flavor than long, slow toasting). Infusing oil is also the way to impart spice, heat, and fragrance to chile oils and chile crisps.

# DASHI

Makes 5 cups

**This classic Japanese stock gets its umami-rich flavors from seaweed and dried fish (bonito) flakes. Drying ingredients concentrates their flavor, and rehydrating them makes for a potent stock that serves as a great foundation to build upon. Use as you would any other stock, such as in soups, stir-fries, or sauces.**

1. Place the kombu and water in a medium saucepan. Turn the heat to medium-low and bring the water almost to a boil, but do not let it boil. Remove the kombu with a slotted spoon and skim off any debris or foam.

2. Bring the liquid to a boil, add the bonito flakes, then turn off the heat. Let sit, uncovered, until the flakes sink to the bottom of the pan, about z1 minute.

3. Strain through a fine-mesh sieve. Dashi will keep for 3 to 5 days in the fridge, and up to 3 weeks in the freezer.

One 4-inch-square piece dried kombu

5 cups (1200 g) water

1 cup (12 g) bonito flakes

# CHICKEN AND SCALLOP HIGH STOCK

干贝鸡汤 | *gān bèi jī tāng* | Makes 8 to 10 cups

**High stock, 高汤 gāo tāng, also known as supreme or master stock, is the foundation for many Chinese dishes. It's a type of clear soup, 清汤 qīng tāng, as the stock is pure and clear. It's the umami starting point for soups, and also used to fortify sauces and stir-fries. Dried scallops, with their funky, ocean-y taste, along with scallions, ginger, and a whole chicken, simmer together, merging their flavors to create a delicious sippable broth. Just a few scallops are needed, because they hold so much flavor that is unlocked when they are reconstituted in the water. You can use this stock as you would any other: to make soup, flavor stir-fries, or incorporate into sauces. Alternatively, season with salt and pepper and serve on its own.**

1. Cover the chicken and scallops with water in a large pot. Bring to a boil and boil for 1 to 2 minutes.

2. Drain off and discard the liquid and transfer the chicken and scallops to a plate. Rinse and clean the pot or switch to a new pot.

3. Smack the scallions, ginger, and star anise with the flat side of a cleaver or knife to loosen their aromatics.

4. Place the chicken, scallops, scallions, ginger, and star anise in the clean pot and cover with about 12 cups (2800 g) water. Bring to a boil, then reduce the heat to low. Add the Shaoxing wine, cover, and simmer very gently for 4 to 5 hours. The stock should be clear, tinted golden brown, and extremely fragrant.

5. Strain through a fine-mesh sieve and discard the solids. Divide the stock among covered containers and refrigerate. As it cools, a layer of fat will collect on the surface—simply scoop it out with a spoon. Refrigerate the fat, covered, to use as a flavorful fat in other dishes. The stock will keep, refrigerated, for up to 3 days or frozen for up to 3 months.

---

1 whole 3- to 4-pound (1360 g to 1820 g) chicken

1½ ounces (45 g) dried scallops

8 scallions, trimmed and halved

5 thin slices ginger

1 piece star anise

¼ cup (60 g) Shaoxing wine

---

**NOTE:** Use dried scallops for umami flavor in stocks like this; you can also incorporate them into rice, dumplings, or stir-fries. Here, the scallops are rehydrated in the process of making the stock. If using them for other purposes, rehydrate first by soaking them in hot water for 30 to 60 minutes, until softened. Store dried scallops in an airtight container in a cool, dry place—I put the remaining dried scallops in a jar in the fridge after I open a bag.

**SUBSTITUTE:** If you don't have access to dried scallops (available in Asian markets), you can use ham or salt pork.

# SCALLION OIL DAIKON SLIVERS

葱油白萝卜丝 | *cōng yóu bái luó bo sī* | Serves 4

**In this versatile side dish, daikon goes through an initial preparation of salting to draw out water and transform the vegetable from firm, crisp matchsticks to more flexible ribbons. This step not only smooths their sharp, raw flavor, but also makes them receptive to the infused scallion oil that flavors them. A drizzle of hot oil is all that's needed to draw out the flavor of the scallions.**

1 large daikon
(about 17½ ounces/500 g)

1 tablespoon kosher salt,
plus more as needed

1 tablespoon sugar

½ teaspoon toasted sesame oil

6 scallions, trimmed and minced

2 tablespoons neutral oil,
such as canola or grapeseed

1. With a vegetable peeler, peel off the fibrous outer skin of the daikon. Slice the daikon into rounds ⅛ to ¼ inch thick, then into matchsticks.

2. Transfer the daikon to a colander and toss with the salt. Let sit for 30 to 45 minutes; the matchsticks will be more pliable and bendy, but still retain a slight crispness. Drain off the expressed water, then squeeze the daikon gently to wring out more water.

3. Transfer the daikon to a serving dish. Add the sugar and a drizzle of sesame oil and toss to coat. Pile the scallions on top of the daikon.

4. Heat the neutral oil in a small saucepan (preferably with a pour spout) over medium-high heat until shimmering; if you place a wooden chopstick in the oil, the oil should bubble around it immediately.

5. Pour the oil in small increments onto the scallions. Try to make contact with all of them.

6. Toss to combine. Adjust the seasonings to taste and serve, or refrigerate until cold.

# ROASTED BONE AND GARLIC STOCK

Makes 6 to 8 cups

**Traditional Chinese stocks always start by blanching the meat to remove the blood and scum, a step that's essential for a clean stock. After that, roasting the ingredients adds an additional layer of caramelly flavor, and simmering for hours extracts the flavor coaxed out by roasting. For a thicker mouthfeel, I like to use bones with lots of collagen, such as knuckles and/or neck bones.**

1. Preheat the oven to 450°F.

2. Put the bones in a large stockpot and cover with cold water. Bring to a boil and boil for 3 to 5 minutes.

3. Drain off the water and rinse the bones. Rinse and clean the stockpot or use another clean one.

4. Put the bones and garlic on a baking sheet and drizzle with olive oil. Roast for 30 minutes, then turn. The bones and garlic should be starting to brown at this point. Add the onion and roast for about another 30 minutes, until deeply brown.

5. Gently and carefully smush the garlic with a spatula so the cloves are peeking out. Transfer the bones, garlic, and onion to the clean pot and add enough water to cover by 1 inch. If you like—and I recommend this—add some hot water to your baking sheet and use a wooden spatula to loosen and scrape up all the caramelly bits; add this to the pot.

6. Bring to a boil, then reduce the heat to low. Add the herbs, red peppercorns, black peppercorns, and Shaoxing wine. Cover with the lid slightly ajar and simmer for at least 3 hours, skimming off the foam periodically. At this point, the stock should be darkened and slightly viscous, thicker than water.

7. Strain the stock through a fine-mesh sieve and discard the bones and aromatics.

8. When the stock cools, a layer of fat will collect on the surface; simply scoop it out with a spoon. Reserve this in a container in the fridge and use as you wish as a flavorful fat. Store the stock in containers. It will keep, refrigerated, for up to 3 days, or frozen for up to 3 months.

2 pounds (910 g) mixed pork and beef bones, such as knuckles and neck bones

2 whole heads garlic, halved crosswise

Extra-virgin olive oil

1 large yellow onion, skin on, halved

1 bunch herb stems (I like thyme and oregano)

½ teaspoon whole red Sichuan peppercorns

½ teaspoon whole black peppercorns

2 tablespoons Shaoxing wine

**NOTE:** Leave the skin on the onion for some color and a bit of extra flavor, but be sure to thoroughly wash it, as sometimes there can be dirt under the outer layer.

# HEARTY BEAN-BROTH UDON NOODLE SOUP

Makes 6 cups bean broth; noodle soup serves 2

**The broth is arguably the most important component of a good noodle soup. For this one, I rely on bean broth, the ultraflavorful liquid that's the best reason to cook dried beans from scratch. Infused with the essence of both the beans and the aromatics they simmer with, the broth has plenty of body since it's thickened by the starch that the simmering beans release.**

## BEAN BROTH

3 tablespoons fat, such as extra-virgin olive oil, duck fat, or lard

1 lemon, halved

2 small yellow onions or 1 large, roughly chopped

8 garlic cloves, peeled

2 ounces (60 g) pancetta, diced

1 small bunch sturdy fresh herbs, such as oregano or thyme

2 dried red Sichuan chile peppers, roughly chopped

2 pieces Parmesan rind (optional)

2 cups (12 ounces/340 g) dried beans such as butter, soaked overnight, then drained

6 cups (1440 g) water, plus more as needed

2 teaspoons kosher salt

1 teaspoon ground black pepper

1 teaspoon light soy sauce

1. **Make the bean broth:** Heat your choice of fat in a large heavy pot, such as a Dutch oven, over medium heat. Place the lemon halves in the pot, cut side down, and let them char, 2 to 3 minutes.

2. Add the onions, garlic, and pancetta and cook until the pancetta has browned and the onions have softened, 5 to 6 minutes.

3. Add your choice of herbs, the dried chile peppers, and the Parmesan rinds (if using). Add the beans and the water; it should comfortably cover them. Add a bit more if necessary. Add the salt, pepper, and soy sauce. Bring to a boil, then reduce the heat to low. Simmer, uncovered, periodically skimming off the scum that rises to the surface, until the beans are cooked through, 1 to 2 hours, depending on the hydration and age of your beans. They should be able to be easily crushed, creamy in texture, but still intact. Discard the lemon halves and herb stems.

4. **Make the soup:** Put 1 teaspoon of the soy sauce, ½ teaspoon of the sugar, and 1½ teaspoons of the butter in each of two bowls.

5. Bring a large pot of water to a boil and cook the noodles according to the package instructions. Add the bok choy to the same pot and cook until bright green and slightly wilted. Drain and divide the udon and bok choy leaves between the bowls.

6. Spoon the broth and beans over the udon in each bowl. I recommend starting with about ¼ cup beans and then just covering the udon with broth, about one full ladle of the beans in broth. Add more as desired. Top with a drizzle of sesame oil, a sprinkle of white pepper, and the scallion and serve.

## UDON SOUP

2 teaspoons light soy sauce, divided

1 teaspoon sugar, divided

1 tablespoon unsalted butter, divided

Two 4-ounce/113 g packages fresh udon

2 or 3 heads baby bok choy (8 ounces/225 g total), base trimmed, leaves separated

Toasted sesame oil

Ground white pepper

1 scallion, trimmed and thinly sliced

# HOT POT–STYLE GLASS NOODLE SOUP

Serves 4

**Hot pot, in which various morsels cook in constantly simmering stock, is a combination of boiling and infusing. Ingredients such as fish balls, tofu, mushrooms, meat, and noodles are cooked in the soup, which takes on their flavors. One of my favorite parts of hot pot is the noodles served with a few scoops of soup, since their strands absorb the soup and become incredibly flavorful. This noodle soup is an easy weeknight hack, without requiring the setup for true hot pot. Start with a fantastic stock or just a miso soup base. Then season it to your taste, throw in some fresh ginger to amplify the zing, and gather the ingredients that will infuse the soup.**

## STOCK

6 cups (1440 g) **Chicken and Scallop High Stock (page 197)** or other stock

Three 1/8-inch-thick slices ginger, crushed with the flat side of a knife

2 teaspoons kosher salt

1 teaspoon light soy sauce

1/2 teaspoon ground white pepper

## HOT POT OPTIONS

Half of a 1-pound (455 g) block tofu (I prefer soft)

7 ounces (200 g) mixed frozen fish balls and fish tofu

3 1/2 ounces (100 g) enoki mushrooms

Handful of dried tofu skins

7 1/2 ounces (212 g) cooked quail eggs, drained

7 ounces (200 g) cabbage, ripped into bite-sized chunks

3 1/2 ounces (100 g) glass noodles

## TOPPINGS

Shacha sauce

Minced garlic

Thinly sliced scallions

**Fried Shallot Chile Crisp (page 207)**

1. **Make the stock:** Put the stock in a clay pot or large saucepan. Bring to a boil and add the ginger, salt, soy sauce, and white pepper. Reduce the heat to medium-low, so that it continues to simmer at a gurgling pace.

2. **Add the options:** Put the tofu, fish balls and fish tofu, mushrooms and tofu skins in the pot and bring to a simmer. Add the quail eggs.

3. Simmer for 5 minutes, then add the cabbage and glass noodles. (I like to cook the noodles in a noodle basket so I can remove them from the stock easily.) Cook until the noodles are soft, about 7 minutes, though this may differ based on brand or type of glass noodles; consult the package.

4. Use a slotted spoon to transfer first the noodles, then the remaining ingredients to individual bowls. Ladle some of the broth into each bowl.

5. **Add the toppings:** Top with the shacha sauce, minced garlic, scallions, and chile crisp, according to your preference. Serve immediately!

**NOTE:** You can choose from a wide list of ingredient options. The key is knowing how long they will take to cook in the stock. For example, enoki mushrooms will cook faster than a sturdier mushroom like shiitake. Cabbage cooks quickly too, but a more delicate green like amaranth cooks even faster. Put robust roots such as daikon in at the start. I start with fish balls, tofu, and sturdier mushrooms, then add greens, canned quail eggs (which are already cooked and just need to be warmed), and finally, the best part of any hot pot: the noodles.

**TO USE A CLAY POT:** A clay pot is an excellent heat-retaining vessel for braising, simmering, or stewing—gentle cooking with a steady, low heat. When using a clay pot on your stove, be careful to avoid extreme temperature changes; otherwise, it may crack. Start with a gradual increase in heat—one way I do this is to first fill my clay pot with hot water and let it sit while I prepare the ingredients. This warms up the pot and preps it for heating.

**NOTES:** You can add ½ teaspoon crushed red Sichuan peppercorns for heat and mala tingling, or ½ teaspoon crushed Sichuan green peppercorns for even greater mala numbing characteristics.

I like to throw two whole dried erjingtiao chiles into a blender and pulse until they're crushed into small flakes, but you can also use red pepper flakes.

Shiitake powder can be bought online or from my favorite local spice shop in Boston, Curio Spice Company.

# FRIED SHALLOT CHILE CRISP

Makes about 2 cups

Chile crisps have exploded in popularity, thanks to the introduction of a number of commercial varieties. The concentrated, infused spicy oil with crispy bits is something you can make at home and customize according to your flavor preferences. The bits can be anything from oats (cookbook author Hetty McKinnon's ingenuity), to fried garlic, to fried shallots. Here, I lean into shallots: the oil is infused with a copious amount of them, so it's more a spicy shallot oil than a chile oil. The key to making it is to keep an eye on the oil, as every stovetop burner's heat level is different. Pay attention to the visual and audible cues given in the recipe. When the shallots are light brown, it's time to remove them, since the residual heat from the oil clinging to them will continue to brown them. Treat this as a punchy condiment: I often will offer a jar of it at the table, with a little spoon tucked into its container for easy scooping. It can add a punch to even just plain rice, though I love to tuck a little in noodles, or over avocado toast or plain scrambled eggs.

1. Peel the shallots, then slice them crosswise thinly and set aside.

2. Combine the gochugaru and red pepper flakes in a heatproof bowl.

3. Heat the oil in a deep pot over medium-low until it reaches 350°F.

4. Add the cassia bark and the star anise to the oil and cook for 2 to 3 minutes, until fragrant. At this point, the bubbling will have subsided around the spices. Use a slotted spoon to remove the spices; discard them.

5. Add the garlic and cook until it just starts to become golden (do not let it burn!), 30 to 90 seconds. Remove the garlic and set it aside in a small bowl. Turn off the heat and let the oil temperature come down to 275°F.

6. Add the shallots to the oil. The oil will bubble rapidly, then subside, so you'll be able to see the shallots clearly. Maintain a gentle bubbling. Add ¼ teaspoon of the kosher salt. Continue to fry the shallots, stirring occasionally, until they are light golden brown, 15 to 25 minutes. Use a slotted spoon to transfer them to a paper towel–lined plate. Immediately add the remaining salt and the sugar to the infused oil left behind, stirring to dissolve completely. Remove from the heat, then stir in the shiitake powder (if using).

7. When the fried shallots are cool enough to handle, roughly chop ¾ cup of them, or use your hand to scrunch lightly. Combine them with the fried minced garlic. Reserve the remaining shallots for your own use (they are fabulous incorporated into fried rice).

8. Bring the infused oil to 250°F.

9. Pour the oil through a fine-mesh sieve over the gochugaru mix. It should sizzle immediately and continue. Let cool to room temperature.

10. Once the oil is cool, stir in the reserved chopped fried shallots and garlic. Store in a covered container in the fridge for up to 3 months.

8 ounces (225 g) shallots (about 6 small to medium)

2 tablespoons gochugaru

2 tablespoons red pepper flakes (see Notes)

2 cups (480 g) neutral oil, such as canola or grapeseed

1 piece cassia bark or 1 cinnamon stick

1 piece star anise

2 tablespoons minced garlic (about 12 medium cloves)

1 strip dried mandarin orange peel

1 teaspoon fennel seeds

1 tablespoon kosher salt, divided

1 teaspoon sugar

1 tablespoon shiitake powder (optional, but a nice boost)

# LEEK CONFIT

Makes about 4 cups; serves 4 to 6

**Confit is the French method of submerging a vegetable or meat in a fat and slowly cooking it over low heat. In this process, the leeks infuse their essence into the oil, becoming so soft they almost dissolve. Leek confit is a great flavor tool to pull out: I toss a spoonful into plain white rice, add it to pasta, incorporate it into dressings or sauces, and use the oil for dipping crusty bread.**

3 pounds (1360 g) leeks (3 large), white and pale green parts sliced crosswise ¼ inch thick and thoroughly washed **(see Note)**

6 scallions, trimmed and chopped into 3-inch sections

1 head garlic, cloves separated and peeled (about 8 medium cloves)

1 cup (240 g) extra-virgin olive oil, plus more as needed

1 teaspoon red pepper flakes

½ teaspoon kosher salt

½ teaspoon freshly ground black pepper

1. Heat the oven to 250°F.

2. Combine the leeks, scallions, and garlic in a 9 by 13-inch baking dish. Add the olive oil. It should cover the alliums. Add the red pepper flakes, salt, and black pepper.

3. Cover the dish tightly with aluminum foil and place on a baking sheet to catch any drips. Bake for 2 hours or until the leeks are melty, falling apart, and soft, and the garlic is easily mashable. Remove from the oven and let sit for 15 minutes before serving.

4. To store, cool completely and pour into an airtight container. The confit will keep in the fridge for up to 1 week.

**NOTE:** Washing the leeks well is a crucial part of their preparation. They can accumulate quite a bit of grit and dirt in between the layers of leaves. First remove the woody outer layers and the root hairs, then rinse the leeks thoroughly at least 3 times in cold water. Slice the leeks, rinse again, and soak in cold water for 10 minutes, so the dirt sinks to the bottom. Rinse thoroughly and drain to remove the excess water.

# TOMATO-GARLIC CONFIT

Makes 4 cups; serves 4 to 6

**This confit is similar to a chile crisp, but instead of being made on the stovetop, it's cooked in the oven at a low temperature for hours to coax out and concentrate the flavors of the tomatoes and garlic. It's delicious with bread, noodles (see Noodles with Tomato-Garlic Confit and Eggs, page 179), or pasta, or warmed up and spooned over rice.**

1. Heat the oven to 300°F.
2. Put the tomatoes and garlic in a 9 by 13-inch or by 7½ by 10½-inch baking pan. Add enough oil to just cover the vegetables. Sprinkle with the red pepper flakes, Sichuan peppercorns, kosher salt, and black pepper and stir to combine.
3. Cover with aluminum foil and place on a baking sheet to catch any spills. Bake until fragrant, the garlic cloves mushy, and the tomatoes wrinkly, 1½ to 2 hours.
4. Remove from the oven and let sit for 10 minutes.
5. Sprinkle with flaky salt and more black pepper. Cool completely before storing in the fridge for up to 1 week.

1 pound (455 g) cherry tomatoes or mixed small tomatoes

3 heads garlic, cloves separated and peeled

2 cups extra-virgin olive oil, plus more as needed

1 tablespoon red pepper flakes

1 teaspoon crushed red Sichuan peppercorns

1 teaspoon kosher salt

¼ teaspoon freshly ground black pepper, plus more for sprinkling

Flaky salt, for sprinkling

**NOTES:** For a flavor-packed but not-spicy confit, omit the red pepper flakes and Sichuan peppercorns.

This is best with in-season tomatoes.

# SCALLION OIL SMASHED POTATOES

Serves 4

**This is one of my favorite tricks to get complex flavor from simple pantry ingredients. I always have scallions on hand, and infusing their flavor into oil is quick and easy. The potatoes are boiled, then smashed, then roasted until crispy. They're delicious on their own, but toss them with the infused oil deepened with black vinegar and soy sauce and they're nothing short of spectacular.**

1 ½ pounds (680 g) small waxy potatoes, such as yellow baby potatoes, Yukon golds, or new potatoes, halved if large

Kosher salt

¼ cup (60 g) neutral oil, such as canola or grapeseed

5 scallions, trimmed and cut into 2-inch slivers, divided

2 garlic cloves, minced

1 tablespoon light soy sauce

2 teaspoons black vinegar

Extra-virgin olive oil

Freshly ground black pepper

1. Heat the oven to 450°F. Line a baking sheet with parchment paper.

2. Put the potatoes in a large pot of salted water. Bring to a boil, then reduce the heat and simmer, uncovered, until they are tender and easily pierced with a knife, 5 to 7 minutes, depending on the size of the potatoes. Drain in a colander and let sit to dry.

3. Meanwhile, heat a heavy-bottomed skillet over medium-low heat. Add the neutral oil and heat until it is shimmering. Add two-thirds of the scallion slivers and reduce the heat so the scallions are quietly sizzling. Cook for 10 to 15 minutes, stirring occasionally, until the scallions have crisped and turned golden brown and the oil is fragrant. Remove the pan from the heat. Scoop out the scallion slivers with a slotted spoon and set aside.

4. Stir the garlic, soy sauce, and black vinegar into the hot oil.

5. Place the potatoes on the prepared baking sheet. Smush them with a flat surface (the underside of a glass works) to about ½ inch thick. Drizzle them with olive oil and season with salt and pepper. Bake for 20 for 25 minutes, until crispy and browned.

6. Carefully remove the baking sheet from the oven. Drizzle half the oil from the scallions over the potatoes, turn the potatoes, then drizzle over the remaining oil.

7. Bake for another 15 minutes or until the potatoes are brown and crispy.

8. Top with the reserved crispy scallion slivers and the remaining fresh scallion slivers, and serve.

# LEMON-CHILE CELTUCE

Serves 2

**Celtuce is one of my favorite vegetables, but it's woefully underutilized. Celtuce stems, large green tapered sticks, are usually sold separately from the leaves, which are called A-choy. The stems are too pungent and spicy to eat raw. The classic way to prepare them is to cut them into ribbons and salt them, then serve with scallions drizzled with sizzling oil. Here, I cut the stem into thin squares, treat them with salt, and marinate them in a lemony dressing of oil infused with shallots and other aromatics. Cutting the stems into squares lets them keep a bit of bite, but if you want a softer mouthfeel, you can cut into slivers.**

1. Remove the woody outer layer of the celtuce with a vegetable peeler or a knife. Cut the stem into 2-inch sections, then cut each section into 1/8- to 1/4-inch-thick rectangles. Some will be narrow rectangles, others will be more like squares.

2. Place the celtuce in a colander and toss with the kosher salt. Let sit for about 1 hour, until the celtuce has lost its rigidity and is softened and bendy.

3. Gently press the celtuce against the colander to squeeze out excess liquid, then place in a serving dish.

4. Combine the sugar, lemon zest and juice, vinegar, and mustard in a small bowl until blended. Add to the celtuce and toss to combine. Sprinkle evenly with the shallot, garlic, sesame seeds, red pepper flakes, and black pepper.

5. Heat the olive oil in a small saucepan (ideally with a pour spout) over medium-high heat. When the oil immediately bubbles when a wooden chopstick is placed in it, pour it over the aromatics in increments, so that every bit of the mix blooms.

6. Season with flaky salt and more black pepper. Serve at room temperature.

2 large celtuce stems (about 1 pound/455 g total)

2 teaspoons kosher salt

1 teaspoon sugar

1/2 teaspoon finely grated lemon zest

Juice of 1 lemon

1 1/2 teaspoons rice vinegar

1/2 teaspoon Dijon mustard

1/2 shallot, sliced crosswise as thin as possible

1 teaspoon minced garlic (about 2 medium cloves)

1 teaspoon sesame seeds

3/4 teaspoon red pepper flakes

1/2 teaspoon freshly ground black pepper, plus more for serving

1/4 cup extra-virgin olive oil

Flaky salt

# BUCATINI WITH CARAMELIZED ALLIUMS AND CORN

Serves 2

**This was born as a pantry supper, something I can easily make on a weeknight. The flavors of shallots and scallions are infused into oil, then emulsified with pasta cooking water and cheese.**

Kosher salt

8 ounces (225 g) bucatini

¼ cup (60 g) extra-virgin olive oil

4 scallions, trimmed and sliced crosswise, white and light green parts separated from the dark green parts

4 garlic cloves, thinly sliced

2 shallots, thinly sliced into half-moons

1½ cups (250 g) corn kernels (fresh or frozen)

¼ teaspoon red pepper flakes

2 tablespoons unsalted butter, cut into pieces

1 tablespoon white (shiro) miso

½ cup (20 g) finely grated Parmesan, plus more for serving

Grated zest and juice of 1 lemon

Flaky salt and freshly ground black pepper

1. Bring a large pot of salted water to a boil, add the pasta, and cook until al dente. Scoop out and reserve 2 cups of the cooking water. Drain the pasta and set aside. Clean out the pot to reuse.

2. Heat the olive oil in the cleaned pot over medium heat until shimmering. Add the white and light green parts of the scallions, the garlic, and the shallots. Turn the heat to high and cook for a minute, then turn the heat down to low and cook for about 15 minutes, stirring occasionally, until the alliums are soft and the oil is fragrant.

3. Add the corn. Increase the heat to medium and cook until the kernels start to brown, 3 to 5 minutes.

4. Stir in the red pepper flakes. Stir in the butter, miso, and 1 cup of the reserved pasta water, and whisk until the miso is broken down and the liquid is emulsified.

5. Add the pasta and use chopsticks to toss and loosen up strands. Add the cheese and toss over low heat, until the cheese is melted and the sauce is creamy. Add more pasta water as needed.

6. Serve immediately with the lemon zest and juice, the dark green parts of the scallions, and some flaky salt and black pepper.

**SUBSTITUTES:** If you have other alliums such as leeks or onions on hand, you can use them instead of or in addition to the scallions and garlic.

You can use another long pasta, such as linguine or spaghetti, in place of the bucatini.

# PAN-SEARED DUCK BREASTS WITH SCALLION-CRISPED RICE

Serves 2

**I learned this method for cooking duck breasts from an article in *Serious Eats* by Sohla El-Waylly, and I've been doing it this way ever since. The timing of these steps will depend on a few things: the power or heat of your burner, the ability of your pan to conduct that heat, and the starting temperature of the duck. So take the times given here with a grain of salt; rely on the visual and audible cues in the recipe and check with a thermometer if you are unsure. Crisping the rice in the scallion-infused rendered duck fat not only coats it in the nutty, toasty allium flavor, but also picks up all the tasty browned bits from the seared duck.**

1. Score the skin on the duck breasts with a sharp knife in a shallow, tight crosshatch pattern.

2. Season with salt all over. Let sit for 15 minutes at room temperature.

3. Lay the duck breasts skin side down in a cold large skillet and set over low heat. Press down with your spatula or a weight, so all the skin comes in contact with the pan. You will begin to hear a hissing sound.

4. Adjust the heat level—low to medium-low—until there is a low, continuous bubbling sound. When the fat has started to render, about 5 minutes into the process, scatter in the scallion shreds. Cook for about 15 minutes total. The edges of the duck breast will have started to change color, and plenty of fat should have rendered out.

5. Increase the heat to medium for 1 minute, and flip the duck breasts, Cook for another 3 minutes, skin side up. The skin should be golden brown and crispy. The interior of the duck breast should be 130°F to 140°F for medium-rare to medium-well doneness.

6. Leaving the scallions in the pan, transfer the duck breasts to a plate and let rest for at least 7 to 8 minutes before slicing.

7. While the duck rests, continue cooking the scallion shreds on low heat until they are browned and crispy, about 5 minutes more. With a slotted spoon, remove them from the pan and set aside.

8. Pour off all but 3 tablespoons of the fat; save it for another dish. Add the rice to the pan and use a spatula to spread it in an even layer, pressing down to compact slightly and ensure full contact with the pan.

9. Increase the heat to medium and cook until the bottom of the rice is lightly golden and crispy, about 5 minutes.

10. Use the spatula to turn the rice cake. (It's OK if it breaks.) Crisp the other side for about 2 minutes.

11. Divide the rice among two serving plates. Slice the duck breast and fan the slices out on top of the rice. Pile the reserved scallion shreds on top and serve.

2 skin-on duck breasts
(6 to 8 ounces/170 to 225 g
each)

Kosher salt

6 scallions, trimmed, chopped
into 1½-inch segments, and
slivered into thin shreds

2 cups (340 g) leftover cooked
rice (from about 1 cup raw rice)

# 腌

*yān*

# PICKLE

Pickling is a practical technique to preserve and extend the shelf life of food. It also transforms the food, and is a potent tool in your cooking kit. Pickles are a staple in Chinese cooking. Tart, crisp, salty pickles are enjoyed on their own, as an appetizer or side dish, or incorporated into dishes as a topping for noodles or rice or to enhance tang in a stir-fry. Long beans, cabbage, mustard greens, mushrooms, radishes—these are pickled in various ways all over China.

Broadly speaking, there are two categories of pickles, based on the content of the brine: salt-based and vinegar-based. The latter is what we know as a quick pickle, where the brine is mostly acidic. This one is really a marination rather than a true fermentation. The former uses a salt-based brine that promotes the process of fermentation, with the resultant acidity a by-product of a chemical reaction. Either way, pickles bring acidity and crunchiness to dishes. They pair particularly well with rich, meaty foods, as in a saucy stir-fry with meat or as a side to a braise.

While there are endless pickling possibilities—worth a whole book, frankly—we're here to talk about the pickles that can be made quickly and easily at home.

## QUICK PICKLE 腌泡 yān pào

This kind of pickle uses acid, salt, and sugar to marinate vegetables in a brine. The vegetables are usually submerged in the brine, and can be ready quickly, as soon as a few hours or a few days. With the use of vinegar, the pH is low (that is, more acidic) to start, which aids in creating the environment needed for preservation. See **Classic Pickled Cabbage (page 225)** or **Quick-Pickled Red Onion with Peppercorns (page 230)** for examples.

## FERMENTATION PICKLE
腌渍 yān zì

The biological process that fermenting relies on is called lactic acid fermentation. Live cultures naturally exist on vegetables and, when combined with salt and water, create lactic acid. The acid kills the bad microorganisms while allowing the good ones to flourish, and also creates the pickles' characteristic tang. The core of the brine is salt and water, with 6 to 8 percent salt content. Beyond that, you can adjust the brine: pure salt brine, 盐腌 yán yān; soy sauce brine, 酱腌 jiàng yān; vinegar brine, 醋腌 cù yān; and wine brine, 醉腌 zuì yān.

An "everlasting brine," one that's used over and over again, is a well-known concept in Chinese cooking. (It's also called "generational brine.") This master brine has the optimal amount of good bacteria, acidity, and saltiness. A tablespoon or two of high-proof white liquor added to the water-based brine helps prevent bad bacteria from growing. It also lends fragrance to the brine and, therefore, to the pickle.

Cleanliness at every point of the process is paramount: You don't want to introduce any unnecessary bacteria into the pickle. Your container should be clean and nonreactive, such as stoneware or glass. Reactive materials to be avoided include aluminum, copper, or iron, which will respond to acid and release unpleasant flavors into the brine. I commonly use glass jars or a special ceramic fermentation pot.

The traditional Chinese fermentation crock is a genius design. It's a large ceramic vessel that features a trough around the top. The lid sits in this trough, and when the trough is filled with water, the water tension seals the crock. Fermentation activity produces gas, which in an ordinary container needs to be released periodically by lifting the lid to prevent explosion. The Chinese crock eliminates this task: as the gas builds, it exerts enough pressure to shift the lid, letting the air burp out naturally. Sarah Kersten Studio makes beautiful fermentation crocks.

# CLASSIC PICKLED CABBAGE

泡菜 | *pào cài* | Makes 6 cups; serves 6 to 8

**I absolutely adore pickled cabbage. You'll often find a little dish containing it on your table in a Sichuan restaurant, to be enjoyed throughout your meal. The salt cure preps the cabbage by drawing out the moisture in the cabbage leaves, wilting them a bit and drying them out, so that once they are submerged in a new solution, they are primed to absorb more liquid. The longer the cabbage sits, the tangier it will be—not only from absorbing the liquid but from the actual fermentation process. This sweet, sour, crunchy pickled cabbage is a perfect crisp side dish to bold, salty dishes, such as the ones you often find in Sichuan.**

1. **Prepare the vegetables:** Chop or hand-tear the cabbage into pieces 2 to 3 inches wide. Place in a large bowl. Add the carrots. Sprinkle with the salt and sugar and toss to thoroughly distribute.

2. Place a heavy object over the vegetables. Let sit for 45 minutes to 1 hour in the fridge to draw out water.

3. **Make the brine:** Meanwhile, bring the water to a boil in a small saucepan with the sugar, stirring to completely dissolve. Remove from the heat and stir in the rice vinegar. Let the liquid cool completely, then stir in the white liquor.

4. Drain and rinse the cabbage and carrots thoroughly. Use your hands to lightly squeeze out any excess water. Combine the cabbage, carrots, chile peppers, and garlic in a clean, large nonreactive container with a lid, such as a pickling jar.

5. Pour the cooled brine over the cabbage mixture; it should be completely covered. Top with a weight, such as a fermentation weight, cleaned rock, or sealed plastic bag filled with water or rice, if necessary.

6. Cover and refrigerate for at least 24 hours before serving. The pickled cabbage will keep in the refrigerator for up to a week.

## VEGETABLES

One small head (2 pounds/910 g) green cabbage

2 carrots, cut into ⅛-inch-thick, 2-inch-long pieces

3 tablespoons kosher salt

1 tablespoon sugar

6 stemmed red Thai chile peppers

3 garlic cloves, peeled

## PICKLE BRINE

2 cups (480 g) water

1 cup (200 g) sugar

1 cup (240 g) rice vinegar

1 teaspoon Chinese high-proof white liquor (**see Note**)

**NOTE:** The white liquor, 高度白酒 *gāo dù bái jiǔ*, a high-proof liquor (40 to 60 proof, up to 80), is important to prevent microbes, as the alcohol will sit on top of the water-based brine. It also contributes a distinctive fragrance, and as all spirits do, helps draw out flavors. You can find it in most Chinese supermarkets—and even Whole Foods—but in a pinch, you can use vodka.

# PICKLED LONG BEANS

酸豆角 | *suān dòu jiǎo* | Makes 6 cups; serves 4 to 6

**Pickled long beans (aka snake beans) are a traditional pickle from the Sichuan and Hunan provinces. The long beans are salted and submerged in a brine until they are tart and wrinkly. The Sichuan peppercorns are not here for heat, but for the citrus accent they add to the brine. The quality of your ingredients plays a crucial role in this recipe. When you open the jar of peppercorns, they should smell fragrant.**

**The beans are traditionally sun-dried before pickling so they become more flexible. If it's not sunny, you can let them wind-dry, but avoid making this on a rainy day since they won't dry enough. Alternatively, you can air-dry them overnight. The surface of the beans should be completely dry.**

1 pound (455 g) Chinese long beans

2 quarts (1820 g) water

½ cup (147 g) kosher salt, divided

1 tablespoon red Sichuan peppercorns

1 piece star anise

12 red Thai chile peppers

8 garlic cloves, peeled

Three or four ⅛-inch-thick slices ginger

2 tablespoons Chinese high-proof white liquor

1. Wash the long beans. Spread them across a drying rack and let them dry in the sun for 2 to 4 hours. The beans will become more flexible and should not crack easily when bent. Trim off the stem end.

2. In a large saucepan, combine the water with 6 tablespoons (110 g) of the salt, the Sichuan peppercorns, and the star anise. Bring to a boil, then reduce the heat to medium-low and simmer for 10 minutes. Remove from the heat and let cool completely.

3. Sprinkle the beans with the remaining 2 tablespoons salt and rub the salt into them. Let sit for another 15 minutes.

4. Curl the long beans into a spiral and place in a clean, large nonreactive container with a lid, such as a pickling jar. Place the Thai chiles, garlic, and ginger on top of the beans. Add the brine, then top with the white liquor. Make sure the vegetables are completely covered; top with a weight, such as a fermentation weight, cleaned rock, or sealed plastic bag filled with water or rice, if necessary.

5. Place the jar in a cool, well-ventilated place. If using a lid, be sure to open the lid every few days to release any gas.

6. Check on the beans after 7 days and taste a piece—it should be sour. If you want the beans to be more sour, keep fermenting them until they are the way you like them, up to 3 weeks. By that point, the fermentation process for these vegetables will be complete, and you'll see minimal fizzing activity. The beans will keep in the refrigerator for up to 6 months.

**NOTES:** You can omit the chile peppers if you want a milder pickle.

The brine can be reused for the next batch of long beans. After 3 or 4 uses, add another tablespoon of white liquor to the pickling solution.

You can use this formula of a 6 to 8 percent salt brine with air-dried vegetables to salt-pickle most vegetables, such as cabbage, mustard greens, cucumbers, radish, or carrot.

# PICKLED LONG BEAN AND GROUND PORK STIR-FRY

酸豆角炒肉末 | *suān dòu jiǎo chǎo ròu mò* | Serves 4

This traditional Hunan dish shows not only how a pickle can be used masterfully in a stir-fry, but also how to stir-fry ground meat, vegetables, and a bold sauce together. The pork is stir-fried first. The key step is to break up the ground meat so there aren't any clumps. The texture should be loose, with partially crispy bits. There is no question that the doubanjiang dominates in terms of flavor, but its spicy, salty, funky flavor is complemented by the soy sauce and sugar. The pickled long beans cut into these strong flavors with a sharpness that makes the overall dish bold and delicious. Cutting the long beans into small pieces gives each bite a pleasant, unified texture.

1. Combine the cornstarch, 2 teaspoons of the soy sauce, and 2 teaspoons of the Shaoxing wine in a medium bowl. Add the pork and stir to combine thoroughly. Let sit for 5 minutes.

2. Heat the oil in a wok or large cast-iron skillet over medium-high heat. Add the pork and stir-fry until broken into small bits, cooked through, and lightly crisped, 3 to 5 minutes. Carefully drain off all but 1 tablespoon of fat.

3. Add the Thai chiles, garlic, and ginger and cook until the garlic is lightly browned, 3 to 5 minutes.

4. Add the doubanjiang, the remaining 1 teaspoon soy sauce, the remaining 4 teaspoons Shaoxing wine, and the sugar and stir to combine. Add the long beans and white pepper and cook, stirring, for a few minutes to heat the long beans through.

5. Serve with plenty of white rice.

2 teaspoons cornstarch

3 teaspoons light soy sauce, divided

6 teaspoons Shaoxing wine, divided

12 ounces (340 g) ground pork

2 tablespoons neutral oil

5 red Thai chile peppers, stemmed and roughly chopped

4 garlic cloves, minced

1 teaspoon minced peeled ginger

1 tablespoon doubanjiang (fermented broad bean paste)

1 tablespoon sugar

10 ounces (300 g) **Pickled Long Beans (page 226)**, drained and chopped into ½-inch pieces (about 2 cups)

½ teaspoon ground white pepper

Cooked white rice

**SUBSTITUTE:** This stir-fry is also good over cooked wheat noodles instead of rice.

# QUICK-PICKLED RED ONION WITH PEPPERCORNS

Makes 2 cups; serves 4 to 6

**This simple method of brine-based pickling is used not only in China but across multiple cultures. The pickled onion takes just 4 hours—or even less. Or you can pickle the onions overnight, or for a few days. The longer they sit in the brine, the sharper they will be. Sichuan peppercorns add a hint of spice and mouth-tingle. Serve pickled onions as a side or use in salads, stir-fries, or pastas. This pickle goes well with salty, bold flavors such as rich meat-based or spicy sauces.**

1 medium red onion (about 8 ounces/225 g), peeled

2 teaspoons red Sichuan peppercorns, slightly crushed

½ cup (120 g) rice vinegar

½ cup (120 g) freshly squeezed lemon juice

¼ cup (50 g) sugar

Pinch of kosher salt

1. Halve the onion lengthwise, then slice it lengthwise into ⅛- to ¼-inch-thick pieces. Place in a clean nonreactive container with a lid, such as a pickling jar, along with the crushed peppercorns.

2. Combine the rice vinegar, lemon juice, sugar, and salt in a liquid measuring cup. Stir to dissolve the sugar and salt.

3. Pour the brine over the onions, cover, and let sit in the fridge for at least 4 hours. The pickled onions will keep in the refrigerator for up to 4 days.

**SUBSTITUTE:** This recipe uses a mix of rice vinegar and lemon juice, but if you don't have lemons, you can use all rice vinegar.

# CHARRED UDON NOODLES WITH BEEF AND PICKLED RED ONION

Serves 4

**Udon are one of my favorite noodles to stir-fry. They're thick and chewy and therefore have the body to be tossed around in a hot wok. The combination of fresh and pickled red onions is what makes this stir-fry. Just a flash of heat transforms the flavor of the raw onion from piquant to sweet. The pickled onions are added near the end, finishing the dish with a touch of acidity and sweetness.**

1. **Make the sauce:** Combine the soy sauce, mirin, sugar, and cornstarch in a medium bowl. Toss the steak in half the sauce, enough to coat the beef, and let sit for 10 to 30 minutes.

2. **Make the stir-fry:** Place the udon in a large heatproof bowl and cover with hot water. Let sit for 5 to 10 minutes until the strands are limber and no longer stiff, stirring once or twice to break up the clumps. Drain, then toss with a drizzle of oil to prevent sticking.

3. Heat a wok or large cast-iron skillet over high heat until a drop of water sizzles on contact. Add 1 tablespoon of the oil. Remove the steak from the marinade (reserve the marinade) with cooking chopsticks and add to the pan in a single layer. Let sit for 2 minutes, then turn to char the other side. Immediately scatter in the raw onion around the beef and let it char alongside.

4. Add the remaining 1 tablespoon oil, the garlic, and ginger and quickly stir-fry until aromatic, about 10 seconds.

5. Add the udon and the reserved sauce and toss to coat the noodles. Use your spatula to spread the mixture in a thin layer so that as much of the surface area as possible is touching the pan. Let char undisturbed for 2 minutes.

6. Toss for 1 to 2 minutes, until the udon are coated in sauce.

7. Add the white pepper and pickled red onion and quickly toss to just combine.

8. Drizzle with the pickle brine, then remove from the heat and transfer to a serving dish. Top with the scallion and serve immediately.

**NOTE:** You can find fresh udon in little square packs in the refrigerated noodle section of Asian markets. They store very well in the refrigerator and just need a bit of hot water to loosen up, ready for a stir-fry.

**SUBSTITUTES:** You can swap out the beef for firm tofu.

You can use skirt steak, tri-tip, or flat iron steak instead of flank steak.

## SAUCE

2 tablespoons dark soy sauce

2 tablespoons mirin

2 tablespoons sugar

1 teaspoon cornstarch

8 ounces (225 g) flank steak, trimmed of excess fat and sliced ¼ inch thick against the grain

## CHARRED UDON STIR-FRY

1 pound (455 g) fresh udon noodles

2 tablespoons neutral oil, such as canola or grapeseed, divided, plus more as needed

½ small (4-ounce/115 g) red onion, sliced through the root into ¼-inch-thick wedges

1 garlic clove, minced

1 teaspoon minced peeled ginger

Pinch of ground white pepper

½ cup **Quick-Pickled Red Onion with Peppercorns (page 230)**, drained, plus 2 tablespoons pickling liquid

1 scallion, trimmed, cut into 2-inch pieces, and julienned

# CITRUSY SOY-PICKLED LOTUS ROOT

Makes 2 to 3 cups; serves 4 to 6

**When cut crosswise, lotus root—the root of a water lily—displays a beautiful pattern. With its floral accent and crispy crunch, it's wonderful in stir-fries. In braises and soups, its texture becomes soft-crunchy. Pickling takes advantage of the root's juicy crispness, enhancing its slight sweetness with a quick soy sauce–based brine. Serve as a crisp complement to a main dish or toss into salads, such as in Pickled Lotus Root and Arugula Salad (page 237).**

One 8-ounce (225 g) lotus root

1¼ teaspoons (7 g) kosher salt, plus more as needed

½ cup (120 g) water

¼ cup (60 g) rice vinegar

½ cup (120 g) light soy sauce

2 red Thai chile peppers, stemmed and roughly chopped

2 strips orange peel (avoid the white pith)

¼ cup (50 g) sugar

3 tablespoons black vinegar

1. Use a vegetable peeler to peel the skin off the lotus root, then slice crosswise ⅛ to ¼ inch thick.

2. Bring a saucepan of water with a pinch of salt to a boil. Meanwhile, prepare an ice water bath. Add the lotus root to the boiling water and blanch for 5 minutes. Transfer the lotus root to the water bath to cool. Drain and transfer to a bowl. Add 1¼ teaspoons kosher salt (about 3% of the weight of the vegetable) and knead briefly by hand. Let sit for 20 minutes.

3. Combine the water, rice vinegar, soy sauce, chile peppers, orange peel, sugar, and 1 teaspoon salt in a medium saucepan over medium-high heat. Stir occasionally until the sugar dissolves and the mixture just comes to a boil. Remove from the heat and cool for 5 minutes.

4. Rinse the lotus root thoroughly under cold water, then drain, squeezing slightly, and transfer to a clean nonreactive container with a lid, such as a pickling jar.

5. Pour the brine over the lotus root. Add the black vinegar and stir to combine. Be sure the lotus root is completely submerged, using a weight (such as a fermentation weight, cleaned rock, or sealed plastic bag filled with water or rice) if necessary.

6. When the liquid is cool, seal the container and store in the fridge for at least 24 hours. The pickled lotus will keep in the refrigerator for up to a week.

# PICKLED LOTUS ROOT AND ARUGULA SALAD

Serves 4

**Juicy, crisp, sweet yet sour, lotus root pairs well with the sharpness of arugula, which is mediated by the sweetness of orange suprêmes. Suprêming the oranges removes their membranes, making a great textural contrast of crisp root and soft fruit.**

1. Suprême the oranges: Cut off the top and bottom of each orange. Stand an orange up on one flat end on a cutting board. Cut down the sides of the orange, following its contour, to remove the peel, pith, and outer membrane. With a small paring knife, cut between the white membranes and remove the orange wedges. Repeat with the remaining orange.

2. Combine the chile crisp, garlic, orange zest, olive oil, rice vinegar, honey, and sesame oil in a small bowl.

3. Put the arugula, lotus root, and orange suprêmes in a serving bowl. Add the dressing and toss to combine. Top with the scallions and flaky salt and pepper to taste, and serve.

2 small oranges (about 3 ounces/85 g each)

1 tablespoon **Fried Shallot Chile Crisp (page 207)** or store-bought chile crisp, stirred well

1 teaspoon minced garlic (about 2 cloves)

1 teaspoon grated orange zest

1 tablespoon extra-virgin olive oil

1 tablespoon rice vinegar

1 teaspoon honey

¼ teaspoon toasted sesame oil

1 packed cup (45 g) arugula

4 ounces (115 g) **Citrusy Soy-Pickled Lotus Root (page 234;** about 7 to 8 pieces), drained

2 scallions, trimmed and minced

Flaky salt and freshly ground black pepper

**SUBSTITUTE:** If you don't have pickled lotus root on hand, this recipe works well with poached lotus root (see steps 1 and 2 of the recipe for **Citrusy Soy-Pickled Lotus Root on page 234).**

# SOY-PICKLED SCALLIONS AND CHILES

Makes about 1½ cups

**In this potent pickle, a variety of chiles are bathed in a soy sauce–based brine. The relationship is mutually beneficial: the flavor of the chiles seeps into the brining liquid, and that liquid pickles the chiles. Enjoy as a side or incorporate into stir-fries, grain bowls, or salads. These are delicious spooned over nachos!**

1 cup (100 g) stemmed, sliced mixed chile peppers, such as Thai chiles, jalapeños, and/or serranos

4 scallions, trimmed and cut into 1-inch sections

1 cup (240 g) rice vinegar

½ cup (120 g) water

¼ cup (60 g) light soy sauce

⅓ cup (65 g) sugar

1 tablespoon kosher salt

4 garlic cloves, peeled and smashed

1. Put the peppers and scallions in a clean nonreactive container with a lid, such as a pickling jar.
2. Bring the vinegar, water, soy sauce, sugar, salt, and garlic to a boil in a small saucepan. Reduce the heat to low and simmer for 5 minutes, stirring occasionally to dissolve the sugar and salt.
3. Remove from the heat and let cool for 5 minutes.
4. Pour the brine over the peppers and scallions. Cool completely, then seal and store in the fridge for at least 24 hours before using. The pickled scallions and chiles will keep in the refrigerator for up to a week.

# FRIED RICE WITH PICKLED CHILES, EGGS, AND SPAM

Serves 4

Fried rice is my go-to pantry meal. When I'm at a loss for what to cook, I make a pot of rice and examine my pantry and fridge for ingredients to add. This is just one possible combination. The rice does not have to be leftover cold rice, a belief you see perpetuated in many recipes. I rarely plan so far in advance and just cook my rice in a rice cooker with a touch less water, so it's on the drier side. Soggy, wet rice never yields a good fried rice, but that doesn't mean you have to use day-old rice. In fact, I prefer freshly cooked, because I don't need to fight to break up a bunch of rice clumps. In this fried rice, spicy pickled scallions and peppers team up with rich, fatty cubes of Spam and scrambled eggs.

The components I look for in a stir-fry are a protein (eggs or pressed tofu are my go-tos); something cured and salty (such as Spam, lap cheong sausage, bacon, or dried shrimp); and something tangy (pickled anything!). The key things to know about each stir-fry ingredient is its moisture content (do you need to wring out the vegetable, or precook it?), its intrinsic taste (chorizo's flavor will dominate, whereas plain tofu will be mild), its texture (crunchy to the point of distraction? avoid mushy ingredients!), and how it will respond in a stir-fry: Will it cook through immediately? Does it need more time? Does it need to be seared first?

1. Swirl 2 tablespoons of the oil in a well-seasoned wok over medium-high heat until shimmering. Add the eggs and quickly scramble into large fluffy curds, just until they are about three-quarters cooked. Set aside in a small bowl.

2. Add the remaining 2 tablespoons oil to the wok. Add the garlic and quickly stir-fry until fragrant. Scoop out and set aside.

3. Add the Spam and spread in a single layer. Let cook until browned, about 3 minutes, then flip and sear the other sides—this doesn't have to be perfectly browned on all 6 sides.

4. Add the soy sauce and sugar and quickly stir-fry to coat the Spam. Add the pickled scallions and chiles and stir-fry to combine. Add the rice and use your spatula to break it up until the grains are loose. Add the eggs and garlic back in, then sprinkle the scallions over the rice. Toss to combine.

5. Add a dash of soy sauce, the salt, and pepper to taste. Adjust the seasonings and serve.

4 tablespoons neutral oil, such as canola or grapeseed, divided

4 large eggs, beaten

3 garlic cloves, minced

Half of a 12-ounce (340 g) tin Spam, diced into bite-sized cubes

1 teaspoon light soy sauce, plus more for seasoning

1 teaspoon sugar

2 tablespoons drained, roughly chopped **Soy-Pickled Scallions and Chiles (page 238)**

2 cups (340 g) cooked, cooled rice (from 1 cup raw rice)

2 scallions, trimmed and thinly sliced

1 teaspoon kosher salt, plus more to taste

Freshly ground black pepper

# MALA SOY-PICKLED RADISHES

Makes 2 cups; serves 4 to 6

**Juicy red radishes get a quick salt-and-sugar cure to mellow them and release some of their moisture, setting them up for pickling. The soy sauce brine is infused with red Sichuan peppercorns (for heat) and green Sichuan peppercorns (for citrusy fragrance and mouth-numbing heat). The quality of your peppercorns is paramount—if they lack flavor, you'll end up with a plain, though still delicious, pickle. Serve as an appetizer or as a refreshing side, especially with rich, salty foods. Enjoy them throughout your meal as a mini side dish.**

2 bunches small radishes, trimmed (about 1 pound/ 455 g total)

1 teaspoon kosher salt

¼ cup plus 1 teaspoon (55 g) sugar, divided

¼ cup (60 g) water

¼ cup (60 g) light soy sauce

¼ cup (60 g) rice vinegar

1 teaspoon crushed red Sichuan peppercorns

½ teaspoon crushed green Sichuan peppercorns

1. Cut the radishes in half. If they are thick, slice into ¼- to ½-inch-thick slices. Toss them with the salt in a medium bowl and let sit for 30 minutes.

2. Transfer the radishes to a colander and rinse off the salt; drain. Return them to the bowl, sprinkle with 1 teaspoon of the sugar, and let sit for another 30 minutes.

3. Drain and rinse the radishes. Place them in a clean, large nonreactive container with a lid, such as a pickling jar.

4. **Make the brine:** Combine the water, soy sauce, rice vinegar, the remaining ¼ cup (50 g) sugar, and the red and green peppercorns in a small saucepan. Bring just to a boil, stirring, then turn off the heat and cool for 5 minutes.

5. Pour the brine into the container. Be sure all the radishes are submerged—use a weight (such as a fermentation weight, cleaned rock, or sealed plastic bag filled with water or rice) if necessary.

6. Cool completely, then seal and refrigerate for at least 48 hours before using. The radishes will keep in the fridge for up to 1 week.

# MISO-CURED SMASHED CUCUMBERS

Makes 3 cups cured cucumbers; serves 4 to 6

**The relatively quick Japanese technique of pickling an ingredient with miso is called misozuke. These miso-cured cucumbers are reminiscent of the Sichuan classic garlic smashed cucumber, which is often used to "open taste"—开胃 *kāi wèi*, a phrase that refers to starting a meal, or stimulating an appetite. They have a deeper, more complex flavor than the Sichuan pickles, since they're topped with a crunchy peanut-chile crisp.**

1. **Cure the cucumbers:** Put a cucumber on your cutting board. Place the flat side of a cleaver or large knife on the cucumber and lightly smash it, smacking the knife with the heel of your hand. The cucumber will begin to split lengthwise. Repeat along the length of the cucumber. Smash the remaining cucumbers the same way.

2. Transfer the cucumber pieces to a colander set over a medium bowl. Sprinkle them with the salt, toss to combine, and let sit for 1 hour.

3. Rinse the cucumbers, squeezing them slightly to wring out the excess water. Pat dry.

4. Smash the garlic cloves with the flat side of a cleaver or knife. Combine the garlic, miso, sugar, and Shaoxing wine or mirin in a medium bowl. Add the cucumbers and toss well to coat them with the miso mixture. Place the cucumbers and miso in a clean, large nonreactive container with a lid, such as a pickling jar. Refrigerate for at least 1 day and up to 30 days. The longer the cucumbers sit, the more complex in flavor they will be, but they will become less crunchy over time.

5. When you're ready to serve, remove the cucumbers from the container and gently wipe off any excess miso. Cut the cucumbers on an angle into bite-sized pieces, 1 to 2 inches long. Place on a serving plate.

6. **Make the vinegar sauce:** Stir the vinegar, soy sauce, garlic, and sugar together in a small bowl.

7. **Make the peanut crisp:** Crush the peanuts into small pieces with the flat side of a cleaver or large knife. Toss them with the red pepper flakes, salt, Sichuan peppercorns, and sesame oil.

8. Drizzle the vinegar sauce over the cucumbers. Top with the peanut crisp and some toasted sesame seeds and scallions, and serve.

**NOTES:** Look for small cucumbers without seeds.

You will have some miso sauce left over. Enjoy it over steamed rice or a warm bowl of congee, or as a sauce with any meal.

**SUBSTITUTE:** I prefer red miso to white for this because it has a higher salt content, but any kind of miso you have on hand will work.

## MISO-CURED CUCUMBERS

1 pound (455 g) small Persian, English, or Japanese cucumbers (about 9)

1 tablespoon kosher salt

8 garlic cloves, peeled

½ cup (145 g) red miso

2 tablespoons sugar

2 tablespoons Shaoxing wine or mirin

## VINEGAR SAUCE

2 tablespoons black vinegar

1 teaspoon light soy sauce

1 clove garlic, finely grated

2 teaspoons sugar

## SPICY PEANUT CRISP

¼ cup (50 g) salted roasted peanuts

1 teaspoon red pepper flakes

½ teaspoon kosher salt

¼ teaspoon coarsely ground red Sichuan peppercorns

1 teaspoon toasted sesame oil

Toasted sesame seeds

Thinly sliced scallion

# 包

*bāo*

# WRAP

Wrapping refers to the act of packaging food in a little parcel before cooking it. It's a large, complex, delightful world, one that encompasses everything from steamed baos to dumplings to stuffed breads. You only have to take a seat at a dim sum restaurant to see the variety, and even that is a small subset of the world of wrapping. In this chapter, I decided to focus on a few techniques near and dear to my heart, ones I believe you can make in your own kitchen.

The most basic elements of these wrapped treats are a wrapper, 皮 *pí*, and a filling, 馅 *xiàn*.

## WRAP 皮 *pí*

The wrapper creates an environment for the filling to steam-cook in, whether it will be baked, pan-fried, or steamed. Literally translated, the word 皮 *pí* means skin. It is an important contribution to the texture of the overall treat, and can also add flavor. The wrapper is usually a flour-based dough, though wrappers in the form of a thin egg omelet, tofu skin, or plant leaves also exist. The wrapper is vital in contributing to the mouthfeel of what you're making. The balance of wrapper to filling is important. Too much filling, and the wrapper may be insubstantial. Too little filling, and the wrapper overpowers.

## FILLING 馅 *xiàn*

The filling is where you can really be creative. What's in the filling will not only dictate flavor but also inform texture and juiciness. It should be simultaneously cohesive, almost approaching a paste, but have enough texture and moisture so that when cooked, the filling emits some 汁 *zhī* (juice). Even before it's cooked, the filling can also dictate how easy it is to handle when wrapping. It's a fine balance to have a filling that is textured but still cohesive, and sweet, salty, spicy, funky— or anything in between. It can't be too dry or too wet. Practice will give you a feel for the right paste-like texture.

Each of the three types of wrapped treats I explore in this chapter exemplifies a different type of wrapper and filling, as well as a different wrapping method.

**Wontons** (馄饨 *hún tún*) are all about the filling, which is wrapped in a thin skin that cooks to become slippery and noodle-like. Their texture lets you slurp them up, just like large bits of noodles, whether in a soup or in a broth.

**Baos** (包子 *bāo zi*) are steamed buns with a filling sealed inside a pleated, fluffy bread-like wrapper. Bao wrappers are leavened and pleated shut, so the technique to wrap these will take longer to master than for wontons. However, the appearance of the pleats has nothing to do with the final taste. Pinch your baos shut or pleat them like a master—regardless, you end up with a delicious bao.

**Breads** (饼 *bǐng;* 面包 *miàn bāo*) are another staple food in the vast world of Chinese cuisine. There's no direct translation for 饼 bǐng. The most common one I've seen is flatbread, but it can refer to bread, flatbread, laminated bread, or pancake. It's really an umbrella term for any pastry made from a dough based on flour and water. Once upon a time, bǐngs were a snack to be enjoyed between meals, but in truth they can also be served with a meal or as a meal. The flaky-layered bǐngs come leavened or unleavened, stuffed or plain. The most famous is scallion pancake, an unleavened pancake stuffed with scallions.

In this section, I share two types of bǐng: the unleavened bǐng, which is more like a pancake, and the leavened da bǐng, reminiscent of a flatbread. The doughs and cooking methods will work with any filling, and I hope they will provide a foundation for you to experiment with.

# PORK AND SHRIMP WONTONS

鲜肉虾仁馄饨 | *xiān ròu xiā rén hún tún* | Makes about 80 wontons

These wontons would be my choice for a last meal. They are also the absolute favorite of my husband, Alex, and a classic. I have vivid memories of making them with my mom when I was a child. In my mind's eye, I see our kitchen: a package or two of wonton wrappers, the plastic wrap ripped open. A small dish of water for sealing. A big bowl of filling, chopsticks protruding from it, ready for the next scoop. A baking sheet lined with parchment paper, filled with perfect wontons (my mom's) and wonky ones (mine).

I make wontons regularly. They freeze well and can be pulled out for a meal without any advance preparation or thawing. I prefer the classic fold, shaped like a gold ingot. My favorite way to serve them is in broth, with a sprinkle of fresh scallions and white pepper. I also love them dipped in or tossed with a black vinegar and soy based sauce.

This recipe is the culmination of years of tweaking and perfecting the seasoning and texture. I hope you find as much delight as I do in both the wrapping process and the resultant dish.

## GINGER-SCALLION WATER

1 cup (240 g) water

2 scallions, trimmed

One ¼-inch-thick slice ginger

## PORK AND SHRIMP WONTONS

1 pound (455 g) peeled, deveined raw shrimp

1½ pounds (680 g) ground pork, on the fattier side

2 teaspoons cornstarch

1½ teaspoons sugar

1 teaspoon kosher salt

1 teaspoon ground white pepper

6 tablespoons light soy sauce

3 tablespoons Shaoxing wine

2 teaspoons toasted sesame oil

*Ingredients Continue*

1. **Make the ginger-scallion water:** Combine the water, scallions, and ginger in a blender and blitz until smooth. Pour through a fine-mesh sieve, reserving the liquid and discarding the solids.

2. **Make the wonton filling:** Finely chop the shrimp, ideally with a cleaver, mashing occasionally with the flat edge so you get a mix of paste and chopped shrimp. Combine the pork, shrimp, ¼ cup of the ginger-scallion water, the sugar, salt, white pepper, soy sauce, Shaoxing wine, and sesame oil, stirring with a wooden spoon or spatula in one direction until the filling is whipped, airy, and resembles a paste. Refrigerate for 30 minutes.

3. **Fill and fold the wontons:** Have a small bowl of water ready. Keep the package of wrappers covered with a cloth while you work. Line a baking sheet with parchment paper. Place about 1 tablespoon filling in the center of a wrapper. Dip your index finger in the water and trace along the edge of the top half of the wrapper to wet it. Bring the bottom half up to the top edge and seal along the edges. Bring the

**NOTES:** Shanghai-style wrappers are thin, square, and eggless, and are sold in the refrigerated section. I always choose the ones that are labeled "Shanghai style, large" on the package—they are bigger than the average wonton wrappers. The larger wrappers provide an ideal wrapper-to-filling ratio. You can, however, use regular-sized wrappers if you can't get the large; use a heaping teaspoon of filling.

It's easiest to chop the shrimp if they are half-frozen.

two bottom corners on the fold side together, sealing them with a dab of water. (See the illustrations.) Place the filled wonton on the prepared baking sheet and repeat with the remaining wrappers and filling. At this point, you can either cook the wontons immediately or freeze them for later. To freeze, cover the wontons loosely with plastic wrap and place the pan in the freezer. Once they're frozen solid, transfer to resealable plastic bags. They will keep for 2 to 3 months.

4. **Cook the fresh wontons:** Bring a large pot of water to a boil. Add a batch of wontons. Stir gently to prevent sticking. Return the water to a brisk simmer, just before a rolling boil, which can damage the wontons. Cook over medium heat for 7 minutes, maintaining the simmer, until the filling is cooked. (I always check one by cutting it in half!)

   **To cook frozen wontons:** Bring a large pot of water to a boil. Add the frozen wontons and stir gently to prevent sticking. Bring back to a boil, add the ½ cup cold water, then return the water to a brisk simmer, just before a rolling boil, and cook for 7 minutes to cook the filling through, stirring gently to prevent sticking.

5. **Serve with sauce:** Combine all the sauce ingredients in a small bowl and stir until the sugar dissolves. Divide the wontons among serving bowls. Spoon sauce over and top with scallions and chile crisp (if using).

6. **Serve the soup:** Place the wontons in serving bowls. Ladle the stock over the wontons and top with white pepper, scallions, and cilantro.

2 packages (16 ounces/455 g each) large, square Shanghai-style (eggless) wonton wrappers

½ cup cold water, if cooking frozen wontons

## WONTONS WITH SAUCE

2 tablespoons black vinegar

2 teaspoons grated garlic

¼ cup light soy sauce

2 tablespoons wonton-cooking water

1 scallion, trimmed and thinly sliced crosswise

1 tablespoon sugar

Chile crisp (optional)

## WONTONS IN SOUP

**Chicken and Scallop High Stock (page 197)** or other stock or broth, heated

Ground white pepper

Finely chopped scallions

Finely chopped cilantro

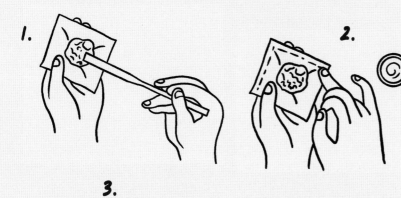

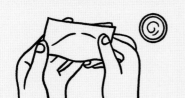

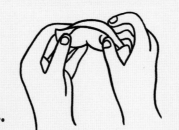

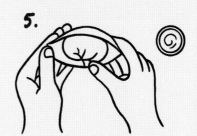

# BAO DOUGH

包子皮 | *bāo zi pí* | Makes enough for 16 large baos

**The recipe for these fluffy, yeast-risen baos that are stuffed with various fillings, such as mushrooms, kimchi, and pork (see page 277), is based off the traditional recipe from my book *My Shanghai*, with a few tweaks. I've omitted the cake flour, since I don't frequently stock it in my pantry, and I've added a touch more sugar and baking powder to keep the buns feather light.**

1½ teaspoons (5 g) active dry yeast

3 tablespoons (35 g) sugar

¾ cup (180 g) warm water, plus up to ¼ cup (60 g) more as needed

2¾ cups (350 g) all-purpose flour

¼ teaspoon kosher salt

2 teaspoons (10 g) baking powder

1 teaspoon extra-virgin olive oil, plus more for the bowl

1. Combine the yeast, sugar, and ¾ cup warm water in a medium bowl. Let sit for a few minutes until foamy bubbles appear, indicating the yeast is active.

2. You can make the dough by hand or with a stand mixer.

   **HAND METHOD:** Mix the flour and salt in a large bowl. Make a well in the center with your hand. Sprinkle the baking powder along the edge of the flour so it gets incorporated last. Gradually stream in the yeast mixture, mixing with chopsticks or a spatula in your other hand. Once all the yeast mixture is in, knead until a loose dough forms. Mix in the olive oil.

   Use your hands to knead the dough until it is soft, elastic, and smooth, 7 to 10 minutes. At this stage, the ball of dough should not stick to your hands or the bowl. If you stretch it, it should offer some resistance and pull back. If it is too tight and dry, add more water, a tablespoon at a time, but be careful not to add too much.

   **STAND MIXER METHOD:** Mix the flour, salt, and baking powder in the bowl of a stand mixer fitted with the dough hook. On low speed, slowly stream in the yeast mixture. When the dough starts to come together, add the olive oil and increase the speed to medium.

   Mix until the dough is smooth, elastic, and pulls away from the sides of the bowl, about 8 minutes. If the dough seems too dry, add more water, a tablespoon at a time.

3. Oil a large bowl. Place the dough in the bowl. Let rise in a warm place, covered, for 45 to 60 minutes, until it has risen to 1½ times its original size. Test it by pulling the edge of the dough from the bowl—you should see a honeycombed, airy, light texture. Punch the dough down and knead vigorously until it is shiny and smooth again, 3 to 5 minutes. The dough is now ready to be folded as directed in the individual recipe.

**NOTE:** Working with dough requires paying attention not only to visual cues but also to tactile ones. The amount of water you need to add and the length of time the dough takes to rise will depend on the humidity and temperature of your kitchen.

# MILK BREAD

汤种牛奶面包 | *tāng zhòng niú nǎi miàn bāo* | Makes 1 loaf or 12 rolls

The soft, fluffy, cloud-like texture and mild flavor of this bread is wonderful by itself as a loaf, but also a perfect foundation for **Sriracha Shrimp Toast (page 91)** and **Mushroom-Scallion Milk Bread Rolls (page 278)**. Tangzhong, a flour-water mix that is cooked to form a roux, helps lock in the bread's moisture, and also increases its shelf life. This recipe is one I've been tweaking for years. It's loosely based on one from the blog *Christine's Recipes,* with proportions, steps, and sugar content adjusted over the years. Use this as you would any soft bread: as toast, or formed into dinner rolls. Sometimes my husband just tears off pieces for a snack.

## TANGZHONG

3 tablespoons (25 g) bread flour

½ cup (120 g) whole milk

## DOUGH

½ cup (120 g) whole milk

1½ teaspoons (5 g) active dry yeast

¼ cup (50 g) sugar

2¾ cups (350 g) bread flour, plus more for dusting

1 teaspoon kosher salt

1 large egg, at room temperature, beaten

4 tablespoons (½ stick/60 g) unsalted butter, cut into ½-inch cubes, at room temperature

Neutral oil, such as canola or grapeseed

## EGG WASH

1 large egg, beaten with a splash of water

1. **Make the tangzhong:** In a small saucepan over low heat, whisk the bread flour with the milk until smooth. Switch to a wooden or flexible spatula and continue to cook, stirring constantly, until a thick paste forms, 2 to 3 minutes. Remove from the heat, transfer to a bowl, and let cool.

2. **Make the dough:** While the tangzhong is cooling, warm the milk in the cleaned saucepan until just warm to the touch but not hot. Remove from the heat, transfer to a separate bowl, and add the yeast and a pinch of the sugar. Whisk to dissolve. Let sit for 3 to 5 minutes, until foamy.

3. Combine the bread flour, the remaining sugar, the salt, and the egg in the bowl of a stand mixer fitted with the dough hook. Add the tangzhong and the yeast-milk mixture and mix on low speed until the dough is shaggy and just starting to come together.

4. Add the butter one piece at a time, making sure each piece is fully incorporated before adding the next.

5. Increase the speed to medium-high and knead, scraping down the side of the bowl when necessary, until the dough is smooth, supple, and slightly sticky, 8 to 10 minutes.

6. Transfer to a lightly floured work surface, tucking the sides under to form a smooth, round ball.

7. Oil a large bowl with neutral oil and place the dough in the bowl. Cover with plastic wrap. Let rise in a warm, draft-free place until doubled in size, 1 to 1½ hours. (Alternatively, let rise in the fridge overnight or for 8 hours. Bring the dough to room temperature before continuing.) At this point, you can divide and fold the dough into rolls according to the recipe on **page 278** or make a single loaf.

8. Oil a 5 by 9-inch loaf pan and line with parchment paper.

9. Divide the dough into three portions. Roll out each portion into a 4-inch-wide oval, then roll up into a log, starting with the short edge, so you have a 4-inch-long log. Place the log sideways, seam side down, in the pan. Repeat with the other two dough portions, placing them in the pan alongside each other, so the bread has the classic three humps.

10. Cover loosely with plastic wrap and let rise in a warm place for 30 to 60 minutes, depending on how warm the environment is, until the logs have doubled in size, with the tops reaching the top edge of the loaf pan.

11. Preheat the oven to 350°F, with a rack in the center. Brush the top of the bread with the egg wash.

12. Bake for 30 to 35 minutes, until the top is golden brown. A thermometer inserted into the center of the loaf should read 190°F. Remove from the oven and let cool in the pan for 10 minutes. Turn the bread out of the pan and set on a wire rack to cool completely before slicing.

# CUMIN LAMB AND POTATO WONTONS

Makes 60 wontons

These wontons are always a big hit with my husband and our friends. The assertive flavor of the lamb is complemented by the warm spice cumin, and the leek confit adds an intense allium hit. The potato makes the filling tender and rounds out the flavors. A fruity balsamic reduction, saved from being too sweet by tingling Sichuan peppercorns, is the perfect counterpoint.

1. **Make the wonton filling:** Boil or steam the potato until fork-tender. Peel, then mash with a fork in a large bowl.

2. Combine the lamb, leek confit and confit oil, mashed potato, ginger-scallion water, soy sauce, Shaoxing wine, sugar, cornstarch, cumin, and white pepper. Using your hands or a spatula, mix thoroughly in one direction until the filling is slightly sticky and paste-like, with no residual liquid visible.

3. **Fill and fold the wontons:** Follow the filling and folding instructions for **Pork and Shrimp Wontons on page 248.**

4. **Make the balsamic-jam sauce:** Combine the water, balsamic vinegar, jam, butter, red pepper flakes, and Sichuan peppercorns in a small saucepan. Bring to a boil over high heat, then turn the heat to low and simmer until reduced and thickened, about 20 minutes. Strain through a fine-mesh sieve and set aside. You should have between ¼ cup and ⅓ cup sauce.

5. Follow the cooking and freezing instructions for **Pork and Shrimp Wontons on page 250.**

6. Divide the wontons between bowls. Spoon 1 to 2 tablespoons of the balsamic sauce over each serving and toss to combine. Top with the scallion and a drizzle of leek confit (if using) and serve.

8 ounces (225 g) russet potato (1 medium or ½ large)

12 ounces (340 g) ground lamb

¼ cup (70 g) **Leek Confit (page 208)**, finely chopped, plus 1 tablespoon leek confit oil

¼ cup (60 g) Ginger-Scallion Water (see **Pork and Shrimp Wontons, page 248**)

2 tablespoons light soy sauce

2 tablespoons Shaoxing wine

2 teaspoons sugar

2 teaspoons cornstarch

1 teaspoon ground cumin

¼ teaspoon ground white pepper

2 packages Shanghai-style wonton wrappers

## BALSAMIC-JAM SAUCE

1 cup (240 g) water

⅓ cup (80 g) balsamic vinegar

2 tablespoons fruit jam, such as blueberry or raspberry

1 tablespoon unsalted butter, melted

1 tablespoon red pepper flakes

½ teaspoon crushed red Sichuan peppercorns

1 scallion, sliced on an angle

Drizzle of finely chopped **Leek Confit (page 210; optional)**

**NOTES:** I always choose the wonton wrappers that are labeled "Shanghai style, large" on the package. They are bigger than the average wonton wrappers, and they have an ideal wrapper-to-filling ratio.

You'll want to avoid making wontons with a skimpy filling, but you should also avoid making them too chubby. The skin is part of the textural experience.

**SUBSTITUTE:** The infused flavors of the leek confit add a lot of depth for just a little effort, but if you're in a hurry, you can substitute ¼ cup (70 g) chopped leeks, fried until softened.

# GARLIC-HONEY FLAKY BǏNG

Makes 4 pancakes

**This dough, which is simply made from flour and water, is modeled on the one for the revered scallion pancakes. It's given a little time to rest so it becomes elastic, and is then folded in a distinctive fashion to create flaky layers. The layers are slathered with a honey-butter roux, creating a savory, sweet, and garlicky bǐng.**

## DOUGH

2⅓ cups plus 1 tablespoon
(300 g) all-purpose flour,
plus more for the work surface

½ teaspoon kosher salt

¾ cup plus 1 tablespoon
(195 g) warm water,
plus more as needed

Neutral cooking oil,
such as canola or grapeseed,
for cooking

## GARLIC–HONEY BUTTER ROUX

4 tablespoons (½ stick / 115 g)
unsalted butter

5 garlic cloves, minced, divided

2 tablespoons honey

Pinch of kosher salt

¼ cup (36 g) all-purpose flour

1. **Make the dough:** Combine the flour and salt in a large bowl or the bowl of a stand mixer. If working by hand, stream in the water, stirring with chopsticks or a spatula in your other hand, and mix until you have a workable dough. Or mix in a stand mixer fitted with the dough hook, on medium speed, until the dough comes together.

2. Knead by hand for 10 minutes, or with the stand mixer on medium speed for 7 to 9 minutes, until the dough is smooth and shiny. If it feels too dry, isn't elastic, or feels crumbly, add more water, 1 teaspoon at a time.

3. Wrap in plastic wrap and let sit at room temperature for 1 hour.

4. **Meanwhile, make the roux:** Melt the butter in a small saucepan over medium-low heat until bubbling and beginning to brown. Add 2 teaspoons of the minced garlic and cook for 2 minutes or until fragrant and pale golden. Remove from the heat and stir in the honey and salt. Whisk in the flour until a paste forms. It should be spreadable and smooth, not clumpy. Set aside in a small bowl. You should have about ½ cup roux.

5. Divide the dough into four pieces, 4 ounces (120 g) each. Work with one piece at a time and keep the remaining dough pieces covered. Roll out the dough into a rectangle about 8 by 12 inches on a lightly floured surface, with a long edge facing you.

6. Spread 1 tablespoon of the roux evenly over the surface, leaving a border of 1 inch. Sprinkle with a quarter (about ¾ teaspoon) of the remaining garlic. Fold the top long edge down two-thirds of the way, then fold the bottom long edge up, as you would a business letter. Spread the top surface with 1½ teaspoons of roux. Starting with a short edge, roll the dough up into a log so you have a fat cylinder. Stand the dough cylinder on its end and press down on it with your palm, so the cylinder is flattened into a disk. Roll out the disk into a 7- to 8-inch-diameter pancake, about ¼ inch thick. Set aside, covered loosely with plastic wrap.

7. Repeat with the remaining dough, roux, and garlic.

8. Heat 2 tablespoons oil in a large nonstick skillet or well-seasoned cast-iron skillet with a lid over medium-high heat. When it's shimmering, slide in a pancake. Cook uncovered for 1 minute, then reduce the heat to low and cover the pan. Cook for about another 2 minutes, until the

bottom is golden brown and starting to flake. (Every burner is different, so watch out for burning and adjust the heat and timing accordingly.) Flip the pancake, re-cover, and cook for another 2 minutes.

9. Remove the lid, increase the heat to medium-high, and cook for 2 minutes more, until crispy on the bottom.

10. Using tongs or two wooden spoons, grasp two opposite sides of the pancake and squeeze them together so the pancake tents up in the middle and releases the layers you've created. Transfer to a platter and keep in a warmed oven.

11. Repeat with the remaining pancakes, adding more oil if the pan looks dry. Serve warm.

# CARAMELIZED SHALLOT DÀ BǏNG

Makes 1 bǐng; serves 6 to 8

**If you love scallion pancakes, you owe it to yourself to try a da bǐng. It's a yeasted, layered pan-fried bread that is crispy outside and soft inside. Here, I veer off from the traditional scallion filling and instead tuck salty, sweet, umami jam-like shallots into those layers, infusing the whole thing with fragrance. This is my favorite version yet.**

## CARAMELIZED SHALLOT FILLING

¼ cup (60 g) extra-virgin olive oil

6 large shallots (about 1 pound / 455 g), thinly sliced

1 tablespoon light soy sauce

## BREAD DOUGH

2 cups (250 g) all-purpose flour, plus more for dusting

Kosher salt

¾ cup (180 g) warm water

2 teaspoons sugar

1½ teaspoons (5 g) active dry yeast

1 tablespoon unsalted butter, melted

Neutral cooking oil, such as canola or grapeseed

Freshly ground black pepper

About ¼ cup (38 g) white sesame seeds

1. **Make the filling:** Heat the olive oil in a heavy-bottomed pot, such as a Dutch oven, over medium-high heat. Add the shallots and cook, stirring often (and more frequently after the first 10 minutes), until they have caramelized and are deep golden brown, 15 to 20 minutes. Adjust the heat as necessary to keep from burning.

2. Add the soy sauce and simmer, stirring, for about 5 minutes, until the foam subsides. Remove from the heat and set aside to cool. You should have about ½ cup caramelized shallots.

3. **Make the dough:** Mix the flour and 1 teaspoon salt in a medium bowl. Combine the warm water and sugar with the yeast in a separate small bowl. Let sit for 5 minutes; foamy bubbles should appear on the surface, indicating the yeast is active.

4. Stream the yeast mixture into the flour mixture slowly, stirring with a pair of chopsticks. When the dough just comes together, add the butter. Mix until a workable dough forms.

5. Use your hands to knead the dough in the bowl until it is smooth and elastic, about 10 minutes. Cover with plastic wrap and let rise for 1½ to 2 hours, until doubled in size.

6. Punch down the dough and knead again on a lightly floured surface for 5 to 7 minutes, until smooth and elastic. Cover with plastic wrap and let rise in a warm place for 20 minutes, until risen again by about half.

7. Turn the dough out onto a lightly floured surface, and with a rolling pin, roll it into a rectangle approximately 12 by 18 inches and ¼ inch thick. Brush the dough with a thin layer of neutral oil, then smear on the caramelized shallot filling, leaving a 1-inch margin all around. Season evenly with ½ teaspoon kosher salt and ¼ teaspoon black pepper. Roll the dough up into a log, starting from one of the long sides. Let rest for 5 minutes.

**SUBSTITUTE:** You can substitute 8 scallions, finely chopped, for the shallots.

8. Starting at the end of the log, roll it into a spiral. Using your hands or a rolling pin, flatten the spiral to a disk about 1 inch thick. (See the illustrations.) Sprinkle some water over the surface and use your hands to spread the moisture. Sprinkle the sesame seeds over the top.

9. Heat 2 tablespoons neutral oil in a large lidded nonstick skillet or Dutch oven over medium-high heat. Carefully transfer the bread to the pan, sesame seed side up. Reduce the heat to low, cover the pan, and cook the bread for 15 minutes or until the pan side is golden brown.

10. Carefully flip the bread, re-cover the pan, and cook for another 10 to 15 minutes or until golden brown.

11. Remove the lid and flip so the sesame seed side is up again and cook for another 5 minutes. Tap the surface of the bread with the tips of your fingers—it should sound hollow.

12. Remove the bread from the pan and slice into 8 wedges. Serve hot.

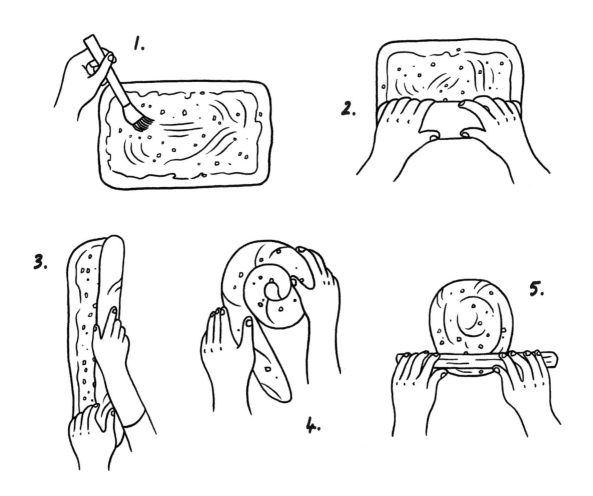

# PAN-FRIED ZA'ATAR FLOWER BUNS

Makes 12 buns

**These little buns are petite enough so you can carry two or three on your morning commute. With the heavenly, earthy fragrance of the spice za'atar permeating the dough, they are inspired by classic flower buns but are made with olive oil rather than pork fat. Don't be intimidated by the shaping—they're just a single knotted strip of dough! Their seasoning is inspired by that in the Lebanese flatbread man'oushe.**

**Bao Dough (page 254)**

2 tablespoons extra-virgin olive oil

2 tablespoons za'atar

1 teaspoon kosher salt

Freshly ground black pepper

2 tablespoons neutral oil, such as canola or grapeseed

½ cup (120 g) water, divided

1. Line a baking sheet with parchment paper.

2. Roll the dough out to a rectangle approximately 8 by 12 inches and about ¼ inch thick. Place it so that a long edge faces you. Brush with 1 tablespoon of the olive oil and sprinkle evenly with 1 tablespoon of the za'atar, ½ teaspoon salt, and some black pepper, leaving a 1-inch margin all around.

3. Fold the long edge down two-thirds of the way and brush it with the remaining 1 tablespoon olive oil. Sprinkle the remaining 1 tablespoon za'atar, ½ teaspoon salt, and more black pepper over the dough. Fold the bottom edge up to cover the seasonings, as you would a business letter, so you have a long rectangle. With your palms, gently press the dough to remove any air bubbles.

4. Cut the dough crosswise into 12 strips.

5. Working with one strip at a time, place a chopstick down the length of the strip in the center and press down, so the edges tilt up around the chopstick. Grab the two ends of the strip and twist into a knot. Place it upright on the prepared baking sheet. (See the illustration.) Repeat with the remaining strips.

6. Cover loosely with plastic wrap and let rise in a warm place for about 20 minutes, until they have risen by almost half.

7. Heat a large nonstick skillet or well-seasoned cast-iron skillet with a lid over medium-high heat. When the pan is hot, reduce the heat to medium-low and add the neutral oil. Place half of the buns in the pan

**NOTES:**
- Za'atar is an earthy, toasty, rich spice blend, usually made of a combination of dried herbs such as oregano and thyme, sumac, toasted sesame seeds, and sometimes dried orange peel. The specific mixture will vary depending on the spice shop or origin.

- You can steam the little buns for 10 to 12 minutes rather than pan-frying them.

- The buns are best eaten immediately, but you can store them in the fridge for up to 3 days or in the freezer for up to 3 months. To reheat, pan-fry again in a small amount of oil, then repeat the steaming process.

2 inches apart and brown the bottoms, 2 to 3 minutes. (Reduce the heat as necessary to keep the buns from burning.)

8. Pour ¼ cup (60 g) of the water around the buns (not over them!), cover tightly, and steam until the water has mostly evaporated, 6 to 7 minutes. The buns will puff.

9. Remove the lid and allow the water to completely evaporate, then transfer the buns to a platter. Repeat with the remaining buns, reducing the heat to low when you brown the bottoms and using the remaining ¼ cup water to steam them. Use more neutral oil and water as needed depending on how many batches you end up cooking (depending on the size of your pan and how many buns fit per batch). Serve right away.

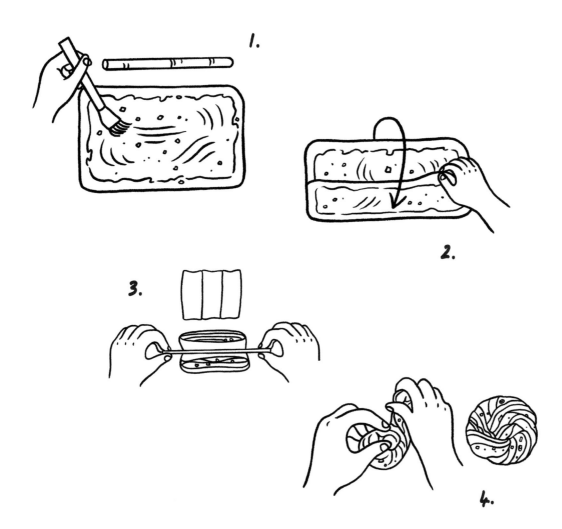

# PORK AND SWEET ONION BAOS

Makes 16 buns

This is my dad's recipe, after I witnessed (and tasted) his many iterations. It's a perfect example of working with the intrinsic properties of ingredients. He was in search of the perfect pork and vegetable filling—one that wasn't mostly pork, as are the traditional pork baos in Shanghai—and that was juicy, slightly sweet, yet savory. He needed a vegetable with a high water content, so that when cooked, it would release its own juices and flavor the filling from within. He tried various vegetables, including eggplant and zucchini, before settling on sweet onion. Adding it last means it doesn't release its liquid too soon, which makes the wrapping process easier and times the release of the juice with the cooking of the baos.

10 ounces (300 g) ground pork

2 tablespoons Shaoxing wine

3 teaspoons hoisin sauce

1 teaspoon minced peeled ginger

1 teaspoon chicken bouillon powder (optional)

1 tablespoon cornstarch

½ teaspoon five-spice powder

Pinch ground cloves

½ teaspoon sugar

½ teaspoon kosher salt

**Bao Dough (page 254)**

All-purpose flour

1 small to medium sweet (Vidalia) onion (6 ounces / 170 g), diced into ¼-inch pieces or finer

1. **Make the filling:** Combine the pork, Shaoxing wine, hoisin sauce, ginger, chicken bouillon powder (if using), cornstarch, five-spice powder, cloves, sugar, and salt in a large bowl and mix with a spatula, stirring in one direction, until all the liquids have been absorbed and the filling is slightly tacky. This will take about five minutes by hand, or you can use the paddle attachment on a stand mixer for 2 to 3 minutes. The filling will be quite homogeneous and paste-like.

2. **Roll out the baos:** Shape the bao dough on a lightly floured surface into a 10-inch-long log with your hands. Divide the log into two portions. Cover one portion with plastic wrap while you work with the other half. Shape the first piece of dough into a log about 8 inches long. Divide crosswise into eight pieces.

3. Keeping the other pieces of dough covered, place one piece cut side down and press down with your palm to form a rough round. With a rolling pin, roll from the outer edge in toward the center, rotating the round as you go, so that the edges are thinner than the center. The round should be 4 to 5 inches in diameter. Cover the round while you repeat with the remaining pieces of dough.

4. Set a bamboo steamer over 2 inches of water in a wok or add 2 inches of water to the bottom of a metal steamer. Cut a piece of parchment paper into a round to fit the steamer and cut small holes in the paper at least 1½ inches apart. Bring the water to a boil, cover, then turn off the heat.

5. Right before filling the baos, fold the onion into the pork mixture.

6. **Fill and pleat the baos:** (See the illustrations on **page 273**.)

    Holding a dough round in your nondominant hand, scoop a heaping tablespoon of filling into the center.

*Recipe Continues*

Using your dominant hand, with your thumb inside the bao and index finger out, pinch an edge.

Working in one direction, make little pleats using your index finger and thumb. At the same time, turn your nondominant hand, which is still cupping the bao, to help move the bao along, so your dominant hand is just pinching and pleating in place. The thumb of your nondominant hand should be pressing down gently on the filling to keep it below the pleats, while your dominant hand is gently pulling the dough up as you are pleating.

Twist the dough together on top, leaving a little steam hole if you can. I like to leave the steam hole, but it's not entirely necessary. It doesn't matter if your pleats aren't perfectly neat; the important thing is to create a seal so that the bao doesn't fall apart. Place the bao in the steamer and repeat with the remaining rounds, placing the baos about 1 ½ inches apart.

You will likely need to steam in batches—if doing so, cook one batch at a time. You can continue to pleat as the first batch is rising in the next step, but just place them in the fridge on a lined baking sheet while you finish the first batch.

7. Cover and let rise for 10 minutes over the hot water.

8. **Steam the baos:** Bring the water in the steamer to a boil over high heat. Once the water is boiling, reduce the heat to medium, and steam for 15 minutes with the lid tightly closed.

9. Remove the lid. Press a fingertip (or the thick part of a chopstick if the steam is robust) onto the top of a bao: if the dough immediately bounces back, it's ready. If not, steam for another 3 to 4 minutes.

10. Serve the baos immediately. They can be cooled and stored in the fridge for up to 3 days or in the freezer for up to 3 months. Re-steam them for 8 minutes or microwave with a damp paper towel on top for 2 to 3 minutes.

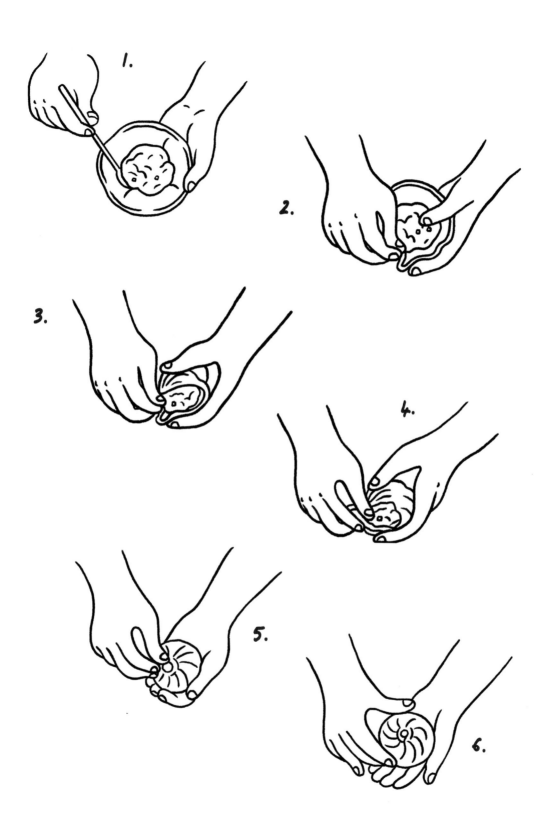

# KIMCHI, MUSHROOM, AND PORK BAOS

Makes 16 baos

Whenever I am in Shanghai, I order pork baos for breakfast. They come freshly steamed in thin plastic bags, and you eat them on the move. The first bite yields a fluffy, soft dough, with piping hot juices. Although the filling is all pork, it's prevented from being too porky by the addition of aromatics. Similarly, for these baos, the richness of the pork and shiitake mushrooms is lightened and brightened by the fermented tang of the kimchi, and its brine mingles with the meaty juices in a fragrant filling.

1. **Make the filling:** Heat the oil in a wok or large cast-iron skillet over high heat until shimmering. Add the scallion and ginger and cook, stirring frequently, until fragrant, about 30 seconds. Add the shiitake mushrooms and stir-fry until they've softened and their juices have been released, 5 to 6 minutes.

2. Add the kimchi and stir-fry until it begins to soften. Transfer to a large bowl and cool completely.

3. Add the kimchi brine, pork, ginger-scallion water, Shaoxing wine, light soy sauce, dark soy sauce, sugar, white pepper, and salt and mix with a spatula, stirring in one direction, until all the liquids have been absorbed and the filling is slightly tacky. Refrigerate until you're ready to fill and shape the baos.

4. Follow steps 2 through 11 of the instructions for **Pork and Sweet Onion Baos on page 272.**

2 tablespoons neutral cooking oil, such as canola or grape-seed

1 scallion, trimmed and minced

½ teaspoon minced peeled ginger

1 cup (100 g) finely chopped shiitake mushroom caps (about 15)

1 cup (200 g) napa cabbage kimchi, drained and chopped, plus 2 tablespoons kimchi brine

10 ounces (300 g) ground pork

2 tablespoons Ginger-Scallion Water (see **Pork and Shrimp Wontons, page 250**)

1 tablespoon Shaoxing wine

1 tablespoon light soy sauce

1 teaspoon dark soy sauce

1 tablespoon sugar

¼ teaspoon ground white pepper

½ teaspoon kosher salt

**Bao Dough (page 254)**

All-purpose flour

# MUSHROOM-SCALLION MILK BREAD ROLLS

Makes 12 rolls

**These rolls are not stuffed with a traditional, scoopable filling. Instead, the mushrooms and scallions are scattered through the dough so their flavor permeates it as it bakes. The bread comes together using a modified laminating technique—not for the shatteringly crispy layers of a croissant, but enough so that the mushrooms and scallions are layered throughout the bread.**

2 tablespoons neutral cooking oil, such as canola or grapeseed, plus more for the baking pan

½ cup (50 g) finely chopped mixed mushrooms, such as shiitake caps and oyster mushrooms

½ teaspoon kosher salt

Freshly ground black pepper

**Milk Bread dough (page 256)**, prepared through step 7

All-purpose flour

½ cup finely minced scallions (approximately 3 scallions)

2 teaspoons shiitake powder (optional)

1 egg, beaten with a splash of water

Flaky salt

1. Heat the oil in a wok or large cast-iron skillet over high heat until shimmering. Add the mushrooms and sauté until softened and browned and their juices have been released, 5 to 6 minutes. Season with the kosher salt and ¼ teaspoon black pepper and set aside to cool completely.

2. Oil a 9 by 13-inch baking pan and line with parchment paper.

3. Place the dough on a lightly floured work surface and stretch it into a rectangle approximately 12 by 18 inches. Scatter the scallions and mushrooms over the dough. Sprinkle with the shiitake powder (if using).

4. Starting with a short edge, loosely roll the dough into a log. Use your palms to flatten it into a rectangle, then use a rolling pin to form a 9 by 13-inch rectangle.

5. Using a bench scraper or knife, cut the dough into four rows by three rows to get 12 equal pieces.

6. Working with one piece at a time, form the dough into a ball by gathering the edges and tucking them under, pinching them together and stretching the top so that it is smooth.

7. Place the rolls about an inch apart in the prepared pan. Cover loosely with plastic wrap and let rise in a warm place until they have doubled in size, 30 to 45 minutes.

8. Preheat the oven to 350°F, with a rack in the center.

9. Brush the tops of the rolls with the egg wash, then sprinkle with flaky salt and pepper. Bake until the tops are golden brown, 20 to 25 minutes.

10. Remove from the oven and let cool in the pan for about 10 minutes. Turn the rolls out of the pan and set on a wire rack to cool further. Serve warm.

**NOTE:** The first step is important to draw out and concentrate the mushroom flavor. Use mushrooms that have a lot of flavor, such as shiitake or oyster. I add shiitake powder for an extra boost, but that is up to you.

# ACKNOWLEDGMENTS

This book is the ultimate culmination of the love, labor, and insights of many. I could not have done this alone.

My family: Alexander Xu, you are forever my partner, taste-tester, technical support, someone I can bounce any and all ideas off of. My parents, Yaqin Zhou and Dongtai Liu, this book yet again, is inspired by you. The taste memories I will always cherish from my childhood are from you. You have shaped the way I cook and experience food. Emmett Xu, my darling son, you're the reason for everything. Lucy Liu, my twin, thank you for always listening to my rants.

Justine Wong, your illustrations give this book whimsy and depth. I adore your work. Thank you for your patience with my crazy concepts and for truly understanding the heart of this book. Your work is going to help readers "get" these techniques!

Berta Treitl: you have always believed in me, pushed me, and helped me strive for excellence. I am grateful for your unwavering support.

The team at Voracious: to this day, I get giddy when thinking about our initial meeting when all I had was a proposal and a vision. That Thanksgiving is one I will never forget! You're the dream team that made this book a reality. Michael Szczerban, you shared my vision immediately and "got" the book. I barely had to explain my concept. I will forever cherish your insights, thoughtfulness, and patience in making this book. Whenever we hopped on a video or phone call, I immediately felt reassured, because you always had a solution. Rux Martin, you are an absolute gem, and you helped me translate my thoughts and ideas to coherent words. Claudia Wu, thank you for helping put this book onto paper with your clean, clear, designs. Jessica Chun, Juliana Horbachevsky, Mike Noon—thank you for believing in *The Chinese Way* and putting up with me! This was truly a group effort.

Caroline Lange, for your meticulous testing, copyediting, and honest feedback in cooking through the entire book! I couldn't do *My Shanghai* without you, and I am so glad you are part of the team for *The Chinese Way.*

Hetty McKinnon, you are my soul sister. I am grateful for your friendship.

And thank you to my readers: for your support, your belief in me, and your enthusiasm to cook Chinese. This book would not be here without you. You have made this a dream come true.

Warmly,
Betty Liu

# INDEX

Note: Page references in *italics* indicate photographs.

Voracious / Little, Brown and Company
Hachette Book Group
1290 Avenue of the Americas, New York, NY 10104
voraciousbooks.com

First Edition: September 2024

Voracious is an imprint of Little, Brown and Company, a division of Hachette Book Group, Inc. The Voracious name and logo are trademarks of Hachette Book Group, Inc.

The Hachette Speakers Bureau provides a wide range of authors for speaking events. To find out more, go to hachettespeakersbureau.com or email HachetteSpeakers@hbgusa.com.

Little, Brown and Company books may be purchased in bulk for business, educational, or promotional use. For information, please contact your local bookseller or the Hachette Book Group Special Markets Department at special.markets@hbgusa.com.

Photographs by Betty Liu

Illustrations by Justine Wong

ISBN 9780316485432
Library of Congress Control Number: 2024938133

10 9 8 7 6 5 4 3 2 1

MOHN

Printed in Germany

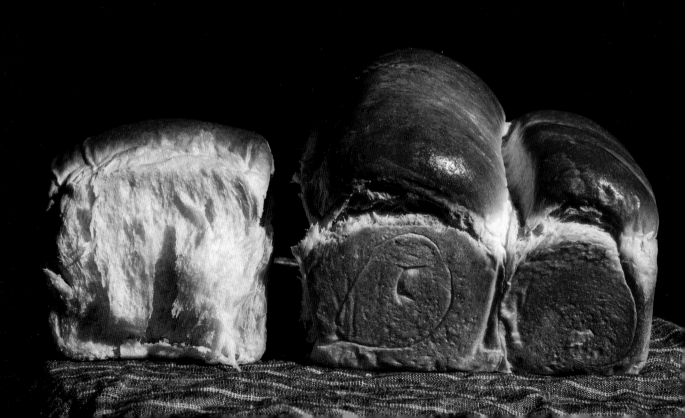